It has been and still is a pleasure to know Natasa and Stuart over the past few years. They are an inspiration not only as a hard working professional couple but as a husband and wife of a family too. As much as their business is a success I see their family is a success too. The things I admire most are their honesty and ethos, their resilience and tenacity, their get up and go which seems endless, and their dedication to serving others.

James Bernard
Business Coach and Mentor, Author of The Bernard Method

Natasa and Stuart are an inspirational couple who are living the dream and show the rest of us that it is possible and how it's done. They set the bar so high that we are compelled to review where we set our own bar for our own aspirations and make some adjustments! They have also become wonderful friends that are giving & sharing as well as a lot of fun. I love the both dearly.

Helen Mitas
Hypnofit, Author of Mindset Dominance

Natasa and Stuart have both been very strong business influences for me over the past two years. Their ability to provide such quality individual business support and advice to myself and others without neglecting the primary family focus of nurturing and developing the relationships with their *young* family is remarkable. Congratulations on creating this fabulous book, I wish it had been written when my children were small.

Megan Wright
Author, Trichologist, Educator, Success Coach and Motivational speaker.

I began working with Natasa and Stuart because I saw they had integrity, warmth, passion, skill in organisation, marketing and bottom line, they have a genuine grounded and openness. I wanted to change the direction of my business. Natasa and Stuart helped me write my 560 page book in just 3 months! I joined them on a 12 month mastermind to take my work from being a therapist into professional speaking, online programs, workshops and retreats. As an author, I have confidence in connecting with lead people in the industry and community. I easily step out of my comfort zone and promote my perspective, doing things I never would have imagined. I speak at national conferences, receive invitations to speak at events, and am involved with a few joint ventures with leaders in their industries.

Anita Bentata
Author, Survivor, Speaker – Activating Artemis – Targeting Relationship Abuse

It has been a privilege to watch and learn from both the entrepreneurial and parenting journey of Natasa and Stuart Denman. Having a family with children of similar ages, and a business dynamic similar to the one I share with my husband, Natasa and Stuart have shown us that you can have a young family and still achieve the business success you desire. Anything is possible, and the proof is in this book!

Rachael Sheldrick from The Workshop Whisperer
Australasia's leading business mentor for self-employed mechanics

Natasa and Stuart Denman are the power-house couple and parents of three little dynamos that talk their talk and walk their talk, every single day with integrity, honor and empathy. If ever you needed an example of a highly successful, happy and united couple running a profitable 7-figure business from home no less, then look no further than the Denmans. Having worked with for both Stuart and Natasa, I've seen the ins and outs and behind the scenes. Hand on heart I can honestly say that they are both model citizens, model parents and model entrepreneurs. When either Stuart or Natasa speak you must listen as you will gain much knowledge, wisdom and insights.
> **Kon Iatrou**
> *Personal Branding Photographer (IKON Images)*

I have known Natasa and Stuart for over three years now and have watched them grow from strength to strength, not only in their business, but as a team. They have developed their own groove in how they manage their roles as entrepreneurs and parents, and they stand true to the testament that you can really have it all. I admire them both individually, and also in how they stand united for their family, and the legacy they leave.
> **Andrea Dix**
> *Your Joy Coach, Author of Permission to Shine*

I have been around Natasa and Stuart for a few years now and every time I go to Melbourne I stay with them so I get to see their every day life with the kids. I have to say I am so so so impressed with the balance they have and how they look after each other. They truly are the most inspiring couple I have ever met, how they juggle their super successful business and 3 kids it's mind blowing. The kids are so polite and happy, I can't wait to put into practice their techniques when I will have my own kids and family. Thank you Natasa and Stuart – you are such an inspiration!
> **Francesca Moi**
> *Empowering Events, Author of Follow Me and Bums on Seats*

Selfishness Recommended

GUILT FREE PARENTS

LOVE YOUR CHILDREN, BUILD YOUR EMPIRE, SATISFY YOUR DESIRES

NATASA DENMAN **STUART DENMAN**

First published by Busybird Publishing 2017
Copyright © 2017 Natasa Denman and Stuart Denman

ISBN
Print: 978-1-925692-13-6
Ebook: 978-1-925692-14-3

Natasa Denman and Stuart Denman have asserted their right under the Copyright, Designs and Patents Act 1988 to be identified as the authors of this work. The information in this book is based on the authors' experiences and opinions. The publisher specifically disclaims responsibility for any adverse consequences, which may result from use of the information contained herein. Permission to use information has been sought by the authors. Any breaches will be rectified in further editions of the book.

All rights reserved. No part of this publication may be reproduced, stored in or introduced into a retrieval system, or transmitted in any form, or by any means (electronic, mechanical, photocopying, recording or otherwise) without the prior written permission of the author. Any person who does any unauthorised act in relation to this publication may be liable to criminal prosecution and civil claims for damages. Enquiries should be made through the publisher.

Cover image: Busybird Publishing
Cover design: Busybird Publishing
Layout and typesetting: Busybird Publishing
Editor: Blaise van Hecke

Busybird Publishing
2/118 Para Road
Montmorency, Victoria
Australia 3094
www.busybird.com.au

Dedication

We dedicate this book to our amazing parents that gave us the gift of life and did the best they could to teach us how to be in the world. It is the blend of great and not so great moments that moulded us into the people we are today.

Secondly, to our three children Judd, Mika & Xara who were the catalyst to become even more responsible, driven and resourceful in life. You teach us new things every day and your love for us is beyond words. We are blessed to have you.

Lastly to all the Parents out there that are doing a fantastic job – Feel the Guilt and do it anyway – the sacrifices for the short terms are worth the lifestyle for the long term.

Contents

Introduction – Written by Natasa Denman	i
1. Boobs, Babies and Business	1
2. Not a Mumzy Mum	13
3. Help is Out There	23
4. Day Job to Entrepreneur	35
5. From Fear to Faith	47
6. Discovering Wealth Through Values	57
7. Six Figures Part Time	69
8. Connecting Through Travel Adventures	81
9. Getting Shit Done Fast	93
10. Leaving Them Home Guilt-Free	103
11. Uncovering New Energy Reserves	115
12. Seven Communication Secrets Revealed	125
Afterword	139
About the Authors	141
Work with the Denmans	147

Introduction – Written by Natasa Denman

Natasa Denman also kept a Journal in the months and days prior and just after becoming a mum and called it Guilt Free Pregnancy – The Raw & Real Denman Journey to Becoming Parents for the First time – Download your copy of this for **FREE** by visiting **www.guiltfreeparents.com.au**

My waters broke in the coaching chair … I was completing my last scheduled session 13 months from the day I started my business. I had only generated $7000 in those first 13 months and any client I had I made the most out of. I had no choice but to keep coaching. Even when my waters broke I got my client to get me my cordless phone so I could ring Stuart upstairs to bring me down a towel. That he did and then I said to Stuart, 'Thanks darl, now go away as we have 30 minutes of our session left!' You may think I am crazy, but nothing was really happening aside from my wet pants … I continued on for a few minutes and then my client and I just laughed, as neither of us could concentrate, and rang the hospital. Mika was born four hours later.

This was the same time I was about to also give birth to my first book – *The 7 Ultimate Secrets to Weight Loss* and needed to do something big to grow a successful coaching practice, otherwise I would need to return to my day job after maternity leave or even earlier as we wouldn't have the funds to support ourselves for me to stay the full twelve months on maternity leave.

I pushed myself to finish the book, to finish my two-year Coaching Diploma in just 11 months and to hopefully finish my day job forever. I had five months to make it work as I was having baby number two that day. For 18 weeks the government would give me paid parental leave that would be able to support us – after that it was back to working for someone else if my business didn't provide the funds for me to remain self-employed.

I had no choice but to continue working out a way to make it as a coach. My back was up against the wall and fitting in breastfeeding around my business was a choice that I made. I also loved my business and clients I was serving so it wasn't hard to try to do it all at once. I could see that some sacrifices would pay off in due course. I had to believe that and practise faith over fear.

Having networked heavily in those first 13 months and writing my first book was the recipe that saw me go from $7000 in the first 12 months to a six figure business the next 12 months. I kept evolving and growing, reaching new levels of success and growth within myself and the business. Stuart was able to quit his day job 2.5 years after I started the business and the last 4.5 years we have been completely on our own. The last three especially we have lived our dream life, moulding it as we please and supporting one another on the entrepreneurial rollercoaster.

Many have observed our journey mostly thanks to Facebook. Many have asked us how we do it all? How do we get to travel four months every year? How do we fit in family time with a 7-figure business we run from home? Well the time has come to unpack all this for you. We feel we have enough experience and a hold on our business and lifestyle to be able to talk about it.

We called this book *Guilt FREE Parents* because it is the core struggle we see with parents on an entrepreneurial journey. The tug of war that they play between choosing to grow a business and grow a family. Many think you can't have it all so they settle for being good at just one. Some put their lives on hold to be the best parent and then suffer from the Empty Nester syndrome once the kids leave home and they feel empty within themselves as they haven't done anything for themselves for decades.

We put the stamp 'Selfishness Recommended' as it's super hard to make things about you only especially when you have children ten or younger. It's hard but not impossible! We discuss how we do this in our lives so that we continue to feel like we matter and we are making a difference in our lives and those of our clients.

Introduction – Written by Natasa Denman

I have struggled many times in the last seven years with guilt, leaving my children behind while I travel interstate and overseas for business and pleasure, but I would not take it back. I have fond memories of it all. Fun times with friends, fun times with family and fun times with clients.

I also decided to add an extra section to this book that is my raw and real journal entries of the days just before I became a mum and when I became a first-time mum to my son Judd. I didn't change anything – left it as it was back then. The way I used to think, talk and how I experienced those early days of becoming a mum. It was interesting for me to read it back as it revealed where I had strengths, where I was vulnerable and how I used to think before my journey into personal development. I didn't realise this but that journal was the true first book I wrote but never published – I found it six months ago on my computer and realised I wrote 30,000 words back then … If you are curious about this part of my journey download it at **www.guiltfreeparents.com.au**.

This book is for parents who run a business and have very young children generally up to school age and at most ten years old. They are in business for themselves and they find it hard to juggle and be successful at the business and parenting side of things. They want to do it all and give their children the best and be an awesome role model for them. These parents also want to fulfil their own dreams and desires when it comes to achieving their goals and making a difference in the world. They struggle with guilt massively and feel torn between the two worlds on daily basis.

This book is for you to enjoy and understand that what you are doing currently as a parent is most likely already amazing and loving. The content in the book will give you extra tips and tricks to improve on what is already awesome. It won't share strategies on how to build your business (check out my other books on this) but more so how to run your life and have a successful business at the same time while reducing the parental guilt we experience. Take whatever makes sense to you and leave the rest.

Stuart's Sections:

Even though we wrote this book together, Stuart and myself wrote the sections on each of the topics completely separately without reading each other's parts. The reason we did this is so we can be fully real, raw and unedited in what was said on each topic from both perspectives – the mother and the father. Most likely the time we will read each others sections is when this book is already in print. If it feels like the sections don't match – this is why … We wanted you, the reader, to get a sense of the male and female perspective on how we approach each topic discussed.

Enjoy the journey into our world and we'd love to hear your thoughts on what you loved – just email us at book@ultimate48hourauthor.com.au

Chapter 1
Boobs, Babies and Business

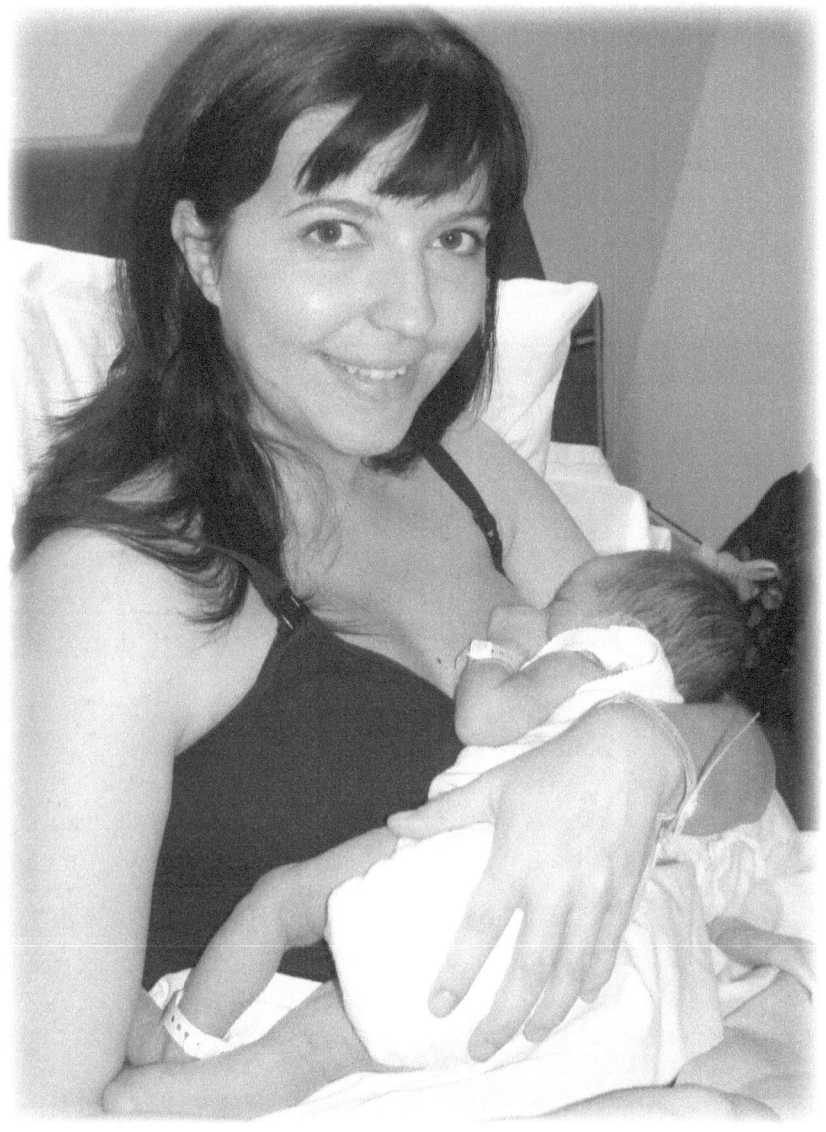

HERS

"Breastfeeding is 90% Determination, 10% Milk Production."
Lactation Connection

To choose to breastfeed or not is an individual decision for every mother. However, breastfeeding can have some hidden benefits for both the baby and the mother in terms of the bonding that you can achieve between yourself and your child and it also gives your child a better start to life and boosts their immune system so they don't require artificial medication or have complications later in life, especially when it comes to the gut.

For me, as well is it being great for the babies, breastfeeding was convenient because it was a lot easier not having bottles to clean and sterilise and it saved quite a lot of time. In saying that, it is a huge commitment time-wise, because you have to be around every three hours for your child. The most beautiful thing though, because you are around so much, you get to bond with your child and it feels super special.

When they reach out for you and nobody else that feeling is the most loving feeling. Their eyes just follow you across the room. Sometimes you can feel like you're this living, breathing, feeding machine, however it is one of the most special moments you can share with your baby.

One of the goals I made when I had my first child was to breastfeed him until he was one year old and that was a goal I had with all three children.

The beauty of breastfeeding is that it does aid in losing that baby weight faster that women put on during pregnancy. However, it also takes a lot of energy and you feel like you need to eat more and drink a lot more fluids. Bottom line is, breastfeeding is the most natural thing that you can do for your child as a mother.

Did you know that many mothers quit, as it is hard and painful to push through and do it successfully? Yes, there are some medical situations where people haven't had enough milk supply, but what I have found when I have discussed this with many other mothers, is that they just could not handle the pain. I certainly was one of those people at the beginning and I had no idea how I was going to get through the first few months, especially when it was in the middle of the night and I was in tears because of so much pain.

If you don't choose to breastfeed certainly you will have more time for yourself, you can be away lot longer and others can completely take over looking after your child. But you do miss out on those special moments and later on there is a possibility that there will be more complications in health for the child.

If you choose to follow this path it is totally possible and achievable so long as you have great organisational skills. The commitment it takes in how you can do it, if this is important to you, is what I'll be sharing in this chapter.

Let's touch on how to get super organised. What happened with me, especially with baby three, Xara, is that I had to travel interstate multiple times during her first year of life. This meant I needed to get super organised. I remember it was mid January when the business year started and she was about eight weeks old. This was still in the very early stages of breastfeeding and required me to be around a lot.

As we were nearing the end of January, and my travel and business needed to get back into the swing of things, I spent the evenings expressing one feed per night. Let's say it was the 10th of January and till about the 24th of January, I managed to stock up to 14 feeds in the freezer. This meant that if I was going to go interstate and travel, that I would have enough feeds, so the baby wouldn't require any formula or anything else outside of what I was providing for her.

This takes consistency and commitment, but it completely works, because if I was going to go away for under 48 hours, then I would have enough feeds left behind so that Stuart would be able to give them to her and then of course upon my return, I would restock the fridge with the milk that I would be expressing as I was on the road. One of the most devastating things that sometimes happened to me is when I would leave the breast milk in some of the hotel fridges and arrive home empty-handed. Those who do or have breastfed know expressing breast milk can be very time consuming and not a very nice task. When you leave behind your 'LIQUID GOLD' it can be very disappointing.

However, I persisted, I got through that year with the third baby being breastfed until she was one and it worked like magic.

If I needed to be away for more than two nights or 48 hours, then I would take Stuart and the baby along with me and I would pop in and out to feed my baby. I remember we were at a four-day convention with the Professional Speakers Association and I was popping in and out from the teaching segments during the lunches and the other breaks to give the baby her feeds.

When I think back, I often ask myself, 'How the hell did I do this?' It was very exhausting as it does require a lot of energy to be there, to turn up and to do all the other things when growing a business. All I had to remember and say to myself is that I just needed to get through 'one feed at a time'. As I said that to myself, I would only focus on that day: What was happening and how I would get my hours organised, over having to think of the big picture and how long I would have to do this for.

I want to touch on here about the pain of breastfeeding, because as I've said before, a lot of mothers can feel like giving up, especially with the first baby. The worst is the first time having this experience and not knowing that there's actually light at the end of the tunnel. For me it was super hard at the beginning. I got breastfeeding nurses coming over to train me, we thought the baby might have been tongue tied because it was just like razors going through my nipples every time my child attached to breastfeed. Many times in the middle of the night I was in tears. I got the blues because of so much pain every single time. All I could think about was that I only have three hours until the next time I'm going to be in a lot of pain.

It was a lot worse than giving birth, because giving birth will come and go in a few hours and you'll recover in a few days to weeks, but breastfeeding was there all the time and for the first two and a half to three months, it was consistently excruciatingly painful.

Being the stubborn woman that I am and one that obviously wanted to give her baby the best start to life, I persisted and thankfully one of the breastfeeding nurses gave me a SUPER tip, which I thought was worth its weight in gold. Ever since then whenever I meet a new mum or a mum who's about to become a mum for the very first time, I always say: 'If you find breastfeeding super difficult and painful, give nipple shields a go'. Nipple shields are little covers that you put over your nipple and your baby feeds through them, so therefore it's not touching the skin (skin to skin is the ideal way) but it does reduce the pain by half, until such time as your nipples harden up and the baby also learns how to properly breastfeed.

A lot of the time the mother doesn't know how to breastfeed properly, because she's a first-time mum. The baby also doesn't know how to do it him/herself (even though they say it's instinctual – they still need to learn). The baby in time will get better and better and more efficient at doing it. If it's not improving then it's a good idea to check if the baby could be tongue-tied, which is where the pain and pinching sensation can be coming from.

I had a similar experience with baby two and three, but not for so long. I was always prepared with my nipple shields with the future births and it took a couple of weeks to adjust to breastfeeding the second and third time around, because I knew that the nipples would need to harden up while the baby was growing in the first few weeks and then I would get used to it. There is light at the end of the tunnel and it's the most enjoyable, easiest and fastest way to look after your child, to bond, to have the skin-to-skin contact. It's just beautiful and cute when they look at you with so much love in their eyes. To avoid sleep deprivation with baby two and three, I slept with my babies until they were sleeping through the night. In the first six months, I would sleep with the baby in the bed. Stuart would sleep in another room for this period, so he would get a full night's sleep and both of us would not need to be zombies the next day.

You've got to do what you've got to do. I would just go from one side to another and whenever the baby woke through the night, I would just attach the baby to the nipple while laying sideways and then continue sleeping. It was very cute to wake up with the baby in the morning, to be able to be there in those moments. This allowed me to keep sleeping, so that I didn't feel exhausted the next day and to be able to continue running my business. I probably could count the number of sleepless nights only on 2–3 fingers, which was so different to the way it was with my first baby. The MAGIC tip that my breastfeeding nurse at the hospital showed me and taught me was that breastfeeding on your side while lying down can be a lot easier. This saved me so many sleepless nights. I don't move a lot in bed so I was never scared that I would squish my baby as some people think can happen.

Those were really awesome tips. So key tips here to remember is to get your nipple shields if you're about to become a mum and use them if you need to, persist and be stubborn, because it's so much easier if you can do this. Learn how to breastfeed laying down sideways, so that you don't end up being sleep deprived.

Then some people ask, how did you travel? What if you needed to be away for too long? Away from the baby? How did you make it all happen? As I said, if I had to be away more than 48 hours in most cases Stuart would come away and we would have our other children looked after by my mum if it was possible. A lot of planning, well ahead of time. We built strategies to allow us to achieve everything and we still did a 7-figure year in that year, even when the third baby was born. I always say that Xara pretty much got raised by Stuart, because I was in and out so much and still committed to my breastfeeding, but I needed to focus, so he was the primary caregiver and I certainly committed to my breastfeeding schedule, but he was the one who was soothing her and putting her to sleep.

This was awesome and wonderful to see as I had that with the first two children. If you don't have enough milk, you can express more and your milk supply will certainly increase and you can ask for some help to do this. When I expressed once a night to get a feed out, I found the more you'd be able to get from your body. Remember to eat lots and drink lots of fluids as your body's working overtime. I have heard mums top up their babies with formula, but I like to think that natural is best, just as we were designed to be. Formula was the last option if I could avoid it.

If you don't have a lot of support or a partner or maybe you're a single mum, childcare centres will still give breast milk to your baby, as long as you provide them with the supply, you can continue working. Just like when I travelled interstate, you can build up your feeds, so that there's 4-5 feeds to leave in the childcare centre for your baby during the day. You pop out into the bathroom, you express it during the times that the baby would need to be fed and then of course you'd provide that day's milk supply the following day to them so that they can give it to the baby and so on. You're always restocking as they're giving it.

The hardest thing is to get the feeds. I would suggest getting 10-20 that are frozen as they are only okay for 2-3 days in the fridge. Once you build up that initial stock then it's really just replacing it, unless you're leaving it behind in hotel rooms and other places. Maybe put a reminder in your phone not to do that in other people's places!

Let's link this to building your business empire:

1. Breastfeeding your baby while building a business is possible and achievable. You just have to choose that you're committed to it 100% and take it one feed at a time.
2. You can be away for up to 48 hours and not miss a feed if you get organised and stock up the freezer.
3. Your baby will not be upset at you whatever you choose. Own your choice and do the best that you can. It's your body after all.

> "The first 3 weeks of breastfeeding are the hardest, after 6 weeks it starts getting easier, by 3 months you feel sorry for mums who have to make formula."
> Lactation Connection

HIS ♂

Simply mention the word 'breasts' and immediately every red-blooded male pays attention. Mention breastfeeding on the other hand, and it is enough to make many men squirm uncomfortably. Before parenthood, breasts are everything but a life-sustaining giver of food for your baby. They are pushed up, taped down, sexualized and everything in between.

To be honest, I hadn't given much thought to breastfeeding as being a mere male, it is purely a spectator sport. I remember Natasa telling me very adamantly that she planned on breastfeeding our babies until they were 12 months old no matter how much it killed her and I must admit, one month into to her breastfeeding, I doubted that she would stick through with her commitment.

This was my first mistake. Okay, it was probably my 53rd by that stage, underestimating the commitment, or some might say stubbornness of one Natasa Denman.

I think most mums have a desire to breastfeed their child. The hospitals certainly push that heavily that 'breast is best' but for many, the experience is nothing short of agony. The chaff and bloodied nipples, the constant pain and troubles with attachment, it is anything but beer and skittles. Yet the alternative was a lot more painful in Natasa's eyes. Mixing formula, warming up bottles, getting up through the night to do these things meant pushing through the uncomfortable phases of breastfeeding.

As the months went on, and Natasa's need for more stimulation than being a stay-at-home mum kept pushing to the surface, she was introduced to Mr. Pumpy (we never did give it a name) so that she could express a feed and start to regain some independence. For you guys out there who haven't witnessed anyone using a breast pump, it isn't a sight for the faint hearted but that is a story for another day.

With feeds being produced and stored in the freezer, I was suddenly more hands-on in the feeding stakes. Nappies and bathing were already old hat and now it was time to master heating bottles and getting our son Judd to take them after being used to the real thing.

There is so much contradictory advice out there about how much milk one feed is, and the best way to feed and burp your baby, it is enough to confuse a Mensa graduate. My advice is do what you think is right and what your baby needs. If they are still hungry after their bottle, give them some more. If they don't want to drink the entire bottle, don't force them. The best piece of advice I can give is that your baby will feed when they are hungry. They don't have emotional eating problems like adults do.

Like everything else, things got easier with time with Judd and very soon we had feeding down like a well-oiled machine and I could give Natasa a break with a night feed if she needed.

On Judd's first birthday, he was cut off. Just like an intoxicated drunk would be refused service at a bar. She had made it to the 12-month mark and celebrated with a can of Jim Beam to mark the occasion.

When I look back, Judd was the easiest 12 months to manage as when baby number two came, the business was really starting to take off. Natasa was coaching more and more clients and we both knew that for the momentum to continue, 12 months of Natasa being a stay-at-home mum (even though we ran a business from home) and being tied to our new baby would be challenge.

I think with baby number two, many things are a blur as you have already been through a lot with baby number one that some of the things that are so fresh in your memory get lost in your memories. Natasa again committed to 12 months of breastfeeding for Mika and the juggle of seeing clients in between feeds, pumping and having a supply built up for emergencies or outings continued.

I have spoken to so many men about their experiences with their partners breastfeeding and many had the same emotions throughout the duration. They felt useless and struggled to feel needed by their baby. I never had those feelings myself as I was so hands-on with everything else I was doing with the kids.

When Natasa and I were talking about having another baby, we agreed that she would again commit to breastfeed for 12 months and I would be the primary carer this time around and the business and Natasa's personal profile had continued to flourish. I had been able to quit my job and I was doing a lot of back end things for our business so I had the time, and desire to be the primary carer for our kids.

We never let the fact that we had three young kids that were all breastfed stop us from doing the things we wanted to do. We travelled extensively, went out on date nights, ran our Author Retreats (with Nat's mum and Xara staying in a nearby house and bringing her for a feed every few hours) and always said yes to any opportunity that would further enhance the business or Natasa's profile.

Don't let things such as babies and breastfeeding stop you from working on your business. Say yes and then find a way. Babies are a breeze to travel with so remember, don't you let Auntie Merle tell you otherwise.

Secret Men's ONLY section

I want to share a few things you can do as a man to help navigate the entire breastfeeding adventures:

1. Never say your partner's 'Tits look HUGE'. Firstly, 'tits' is not a word that any woman I know particularly likes and secondly, they are fully aware that their breast are engorged with milk and most of the time don't feel very comfortable about it.

2. Just because your partner's breasts are bigger, it doesn't mean that they want you to fondle them at every opportunity. In fact, they very well might want you to stay well away – just be okay with that!

3. If your partner has had a rough night with feeding if your baby is unsettled, make sure you give her a break when you can. Lack of sleep is something that makes any of us cranky and tired. Do your bit; it is your baby too!

4. Don't ask to taste your partner's breast milk. They think that kind of stuff is disgusting – if you really want to have a taste, sneak one in when she isn't looking.

5. You will get vomited on, so get used to it. We were blessed to have all three babies happy and healthy and not suffer from reflux or gastric problems yet still had to deal with the occasional vomiting episode. The best piece of advice I can give here is keep your mouth shut at all times when holding your baby above your head … Oh, and not all babies burp so don't slap their backs for hours after a feed. None of our kids burped – fact.

Chapter 2
Not a Mumzy Mum

HERS ♀

> "I used to hate flight time and delays before becoming a mum, now that I have 3 kids I enjoy the luxury of uninterrupted time on planes and waiting in the lounge. It's when I get the most done and am just me."
> Natasa Denman

My mum left me in Macedonia at the age of 11 and a half. She could foresee that the future in Macedonia did not look so bright for herself or me so she decided to look for a better life elsewhere. We ended up being separated for two and a half years until I was 14. I didn't know it at the time but my mum always worked very hard especially since she was a single parent.

Back then there was no Skype or Face Time. We got to speak on the phone twice a year for a few minutes as it was very expensive. I used to dream that she was with me and we were together having fun like we used to. But then I would wake up and realise that it wasn't real. Now that I am a parent myself, I have no idea how she lasted so long without seeing me. What I also realise is that she had the foresight to know that a period of sacrifice is usually followed by benefits that last a lifetime.

My mum was not a mumzy mum. She worked three jobs and would go away for a month at a time in Greece to make some extra cash during the summers so she can provide a great lifestyle for us. She worked hard to figure out a way to get us out of a poverty stricken country to one that would give us both opportunities we could only dream of in Macedonia.

This separation was beneficial for me as well. At the time it was the worst feeling in the world, but being on my own (as my dad was not really a caregiver to me) enabled me to build on two very important traits – INDEPENDENCE AND RESILIENCE! These are the two traits that nowadays give me the strength and courage to run my business and make decisions in life that will be of benefit to me, my family and the greater community I am in.

There are some benefits to not being a Mumzy mum:

- You will be more successful in your business as you will devote more time there.
- Your children will learn different skills from you.
- You will show your children how to chase their dreams and create a life by design.
- Your children will benefit from the resources you will be able provide.
- You will pass on the traits of Independence and Resilience to your children.

What I have found in a lot of my workshops, trainings and retreats is that women are ashamed to admit that they are not a mumzy mum!

Let's first define this – A person who is not a mumzy mum is generally more driven by her goals, career and vision to build something bigger then herself and the immediate family. She loves her children and she loves to know she can contribute on a bigger scale. She is not really the sit-on-the-floor-and-play-for-hours kind of person. She is also not a person who may always be at the schoolyard dropping off and picking up the kids. Most of the other parents in the schoolyard probably don't know her as she comes in and out at random times. She often outsources household tasks to others who love to do it so she can focus on building her empire. She has a vision that when she helps others achieve their dreams, hers and her family's dreams will be taken care of. She may need to travel a bit for business. She feels guilty leaving the family, but also knows this is going be good for everyone in the end. She also knows on her trips she gets to focus and be very productive and enjoy a bit of 'me' time while away. She is determined, stubborn and driven. She will choose the business first but drop everything if there is an emergency. Her values may not have family at the top but that doesn't mean she doesn't love them the most.

Some of the setbacks to not being a mumzy mum is that you may miss some of the kids stuff e.g. a concerts or a special day (but not all of it if you get organised) and it may sometimes feel like the kids prefer the 'nurturer' parent.

I want to share with you here some strategies on how to be okay with not being a mumzy mum:

1. Understand it's not something to a be ashamed of
2. Think Quality over Quantity
3. Think Opportunities.

Lets break this down ...

It's Not Shameful

How do I know this? I often describe myself in my seminars as not being a mumzy mum. When I say it and explain it I see lots of heads nodding. I see them agreeing with me and coming up to me after the seminar to confess that they are also like that. By admitting this, it gives permission to others to be like that too. Understand it is okay if you are like this also. We are all different. To fulfil our highest purpose we must operate in our highest values otherwise we will develop diseases and illnesses, which are just signs that we are not on the right path. Own your style as you biggest wealth is hidden in what you value most.

Think Quality Over Quantity

When I had my first baby, Judd, I didn't have my business. I was on true maternity leave for 12 months. Once I got through the first three months of getting used to being a parent and set a routine, I became very bored and discontent. I was feeling like I was wasting my life away. Babies are not very interactive and I couldn't just play with rattles and blocks for hours on end. I would count the minutes and hours until Stuart came home so I could go somewhere else and have some time for me. Nowadays I know

I am not a mumzy mum that would take the kids to a million and one activities and fill up all my time with their stuff. So I have the motto, 'Work Hard Play Hard'. This means I am fulfilled building my empire, which also tires me out but it's rewarding. When I get to that point of too much work I always schedule a ton of time to play with the family. Nowadays we take four months off in a year and work hard for eight. We still have every weekend as a three-day weekend. The first four days of the week as focused work – no excuses – when we get everything done. This way we get Quality time over a balance of hours each day.

Think Opportunities

When you are not a mumzy mum, you will devote more time to your empire meaning you are more likely to be more successful. In turn this provides the resources to enable you to give your children a great education, the ability to role-model success and determination, consistency and action. You will also be able to say *Yes* to opportunities without guilt and live a fulfilled life yourself. I say to other mums, fast forward to the future and imagine who your child will be as an adult. In most cases they will be modelling the life you are living right now. If you are sacrificing yourself all the time and putting them first always they will be in the same boat too. If you want your children to chase their dreams, build their lives as they choose, make sure you model the same for them too.

Not being a mumzy mum won't make your children love you any less. They won't really know any different. The most important thing is to make sure you stick to any promises you make, that you plan well ahead of time your work and play time with them so you have things to look forward to together and take the time to talk to them one-on-one. We have dinner together as a family 90% of time and sit together in one place to check in with one another about how our days have been.

Your life will be so much more colourful and happy when you own your strengths. Not all mums were made equal and the mum flavour you choose to be will be the perfect one for your kids. After all, they chose you to be their parent because they need to learn a certain lesson that only you can teach them.

Let's link this to Building Your Business Empire:

1. Not being a Mumzy Mum does not mean you are not an Amazing Mum to your children.
2. Not being a mumzy mum will allow you to be more successful in business.
3. Your children will learn other skills and perhaps take over or help you in your business in due course.

"Focus on what you can control, forgive yourself for what you can't."
　　Overheard at Working Mum of the Year Awards

HIS

I remember watching old TV shows from the 60s and the classic stereotypical women who played the roles of mum and homemaker. I knew from very early on that I didn't marry one of these women. Even though Natasa was obsessed with cleanliness and organization in our homes we lived in until our first child was born, homemaking wasn't going to be her thing.

I think it changes for many people when they have children. The things that used to matter don't really matter anymore such as non-matching tea towels, a cup left in the sink and uneven hand towels hung in the bathroom.

What I have found in life is that there are people who are organized, and people who aren't. The organized ones are able to make the most of their time as they prioritize what needs to get done and let go of the things that aren't important.

When Judd was born, I had just started working at my SpecSavers business that I had bought into as a partner so I was away for 50 hours a week, which meant that Natasa was at home caring for Judd. Now, Natasa is one of those organized people I mentioned earlier so very soon boredom was a big factor in her everyday life. Although she loved Judd very deeply, newborns are really pretty boring, and I say that with open honesty.

They sleep, they cry, they feed repeat. Every day is like Ground Hog day and as we have always had minimalist design throughout our houses, there wasn't much to do except wish for some stimulation. Some days as I walked into the house I was handed Judd and told, "Here is 'YOUR' son, he needs a bath".

As time went by and Judd started being more interactive I could see that Natasa got more enjoyment out of the interaction but unlike me, she couldn't just sit and play on the carpet with him for hours. This has continued on with our subsequent two children and unlike most of her mums from her mothers' groups and friends who have become mums at roughly the same time as ourselves, Natasa hasn't fallen into wanting to become a true stay-at-home mum and have our children dominate her life.

We don't have traditional roles in our family and once you know our individual values it won't surprise you at all. My two highest values are family and quality time while Natasa's are contribution and significance. Me being the primary carer of our children makes sense and it works so well as Natasa and I both get to have our values taken care of. I have had several people, usually men, ask me if I assumed my role because I was forced to and the honest answer is NO. One of the biggest issues many couples face is that they are fulfilling roles that bring them no joy. This causes resentment and anger to build up.

As I mentioned in the last chapter, the only reason we agreed to have our third child was if I wanted to raise another baby and child. Natasa loved her life with the ability to run her business as she wanted, knowing that I was keeping the family side of things running.

Another assumption that people make is that Natasa isn't hands-on with our kids. This is nothing further from the truth. She is involved in every aspect of their lives and gives them one of the best gifts she can give them, and that is an empowered, passionate, focused role model.

Our children are growing up watching what a healthy relationship looks like that is filled with love, understanding and teamwork. I want Judd to be a hands-on dad when he grows up and learn to cook and look after himself so he can be independent. I want Mika and Xara to grow up believing that as a woman, you can be strong, focused yet feminine at the same time.

The decision that we make as a couple is what we understand to be the best for our family and don't worry about what others might think. My father continues to make comments and has for the past four years. Off the cuff remarks like, "Will the kids remember what you look like" when Natasa is heading off on a weeks tour running her workshops and, "There you go leaving your family again" and it no longer upsets us like it did.

His belief must be that the woman's role is at home as a mum, which is interesting as he separated from my mum when I was eight years old and therefore never raised me as he worked all of the time when I was little and then wasn't around through my developmental years.

The biggest takeaway I want you to get from reading this chapter is adopting the belief that as long as your values are being met, and you keep the lines of communication open between you and your partner, if you need a 'chop out' in a role that is yours and teamwork is always committed to, you can live a life being happy and fulfilled, even if it means mastering hospital corners on your bed sheets.

Secret Men's Only Section

I want to share some tips to help you navigate around traditional roles and what a 'mum' is supposed to do:

1. Never, and I mean never, say that staying at home with the kids all day would be like a holiday – it isn't and will get you in the doghouse for a month.

2. Learn to change a nappy while holding your breath – when done right, and with military precision, you can get it done in 30 seconds.

3. Kids have really cool toys and we get to play with them and invent crazy games that keep us occupied for hours. The more you seem to be engaged with your children playing some wonderful adventure, the less likely you are to be asked to do something less fun, like match 70 socks out of the washing at the end of the week.

4. If you are better than your partner at a certain role, but they do it just because they feel obligated to, offer to take it over for them especially if you know they hate doing it – happy wife, happy life.

5. Never criticize the way your partner does something unless you have an idea how you can make it work better. And if it is just a theory, or your belief that doing it your way will be better for your family, actually do it yourself and make sure that you are right before bringing up the suggestion. Women hate being told that they are wrong, just saying …

Chapter 3
Help is Out There

HERS

"Ask for help not because you're weak, but because you want to remain strong."
Les Brown

One of the biggest challenges we soon realised when we have our first child is the fact they need to be looked after 24/7 by an adult for at least the first ten years of their life, if not more. You certainly can't leave a ten-year old at home even though they are a lot more independent and less needing of childcare.

The beauty of childcare is that as an entrepreneur, it does give you the luxury of having that time to focus fully on your business, which means that your productivity will increase, you'll become a lot more effective and you'll get a lot more done in less time without distractions.

When your children are in childcare, it does remove the guilt when you know they're being taken care of and you're investing in that with professionals. Therefore you should be doing things to build your business and therefore be able to afford to have them in childcare and for you to be fulfilling and living and satisfying your desires.

At the end of the day when I had my first child, I had quite a lot of maternity leave. I didn't have the business at the time and I started to realise after 6-7 months that I wasn't going to be a 'mumzy mum' or 'stay at home mum'. I felt that the time was more like quantity time and not quality time.

That's why nowadays I focus on quality over quantity and I really enjoy a lot more being around my children when I know that the other things have been taken care of and my other desires and things that I need to fulfil myself and my life have also been completed and achieved.

Childcare is not only good for running your business and being able to have focus in it without distraction, but it's also good for your child as it builds their social skills and their interaction with other people. I have found that children who have never been in childcare can be a lot more shy when interacting with others when they start school, whereas those who have been in childcare and kindergarten are a lot more confident and know how to interact in group situations.

When I had my very first baby, the maternal and child health nurse said to me that if you want to have the most influence over your child's behaviour and beliefs and values, she said that having them in care no more than three days per week would enable me to be the biggest influencer and hence my child's primary influencer in their life.

That's what I chose to do and I continue to do, our third child is still in childcare while we're writing this book and she does Tuesdays, Wednesdays and Thursdays, which is what all of our children did.

If you choose not to have your child in childcare and be that primary caregiver until they start school, it can be a little bit of a messy time. There will be a lot of distractions, you might feel guilty that you're not spending time with your child at home and that you need to focus on activities that are required for you to build your business. It would become quite hard to organise to attend meetings and networking and different appointments and then potentially your child could struggle when they do begin in school if not adjusted.

I'm going to talk about what kind of childcare there is and what kind of support you can get whether it is paid or free:

1. Your partner support
2. Parents and/or friends
3. Childcare options: family day care or purely childcare centres.

Let's look at these three in a little bit more detail.

With your partner (I know you may be a single mum, but let's pretend that you do have a partner for the sake of this exercise) you need to work out does your partner have a regular roster with their job or career? When I had baby number one and baby number two, Stuart was still working in the retail management industry, so he did have a set monthly roster. I had to work around his roster and then he would come home and would take over their care and I would do a lot of coaching late in the evenings and we would plan weeks in advance and have a lot of communication around what was coming up and how we were going to juggle that with childcare.

We were very lucky in those early days also to have our child in two different childcare centres, which allowed us to have a little bit more flexibility that allowed us to be a lot more ad hoc. If you can find a sweet deal like that when a childcare centre would allow you to put your child in different days each week, such as this week on a Tuesday, next week on a Friday or whatever suits you as having more flexibility earlier on in your business worked really well.

At the centre we used they changed the rules after 12 months and then we had to stick to our Tuesday, Wednesday and Thursday schedule, which meant we weren't using our time to the best we could.

Then you need to access parents or if you don't have them around, your friends, because sometimes I know that not everyone has their parents around and I understand that. There are a lot of people other than your own parents who have children and if you ask well ahead of time, they can look after your kids. This is super important to get help with, even if you need to ask sometimes 1-2 months ahead of time and then when you have carers locked in, have your systems and instructions written down, so that they know exactly how to help you looking after your child. Then confirm 1-2 weeks before that day approaches and certainly reward those people who are helping you by doing vice versa, looking after their children when they need it. Leave some cash for entertainment and for them looking after your child, a little unexpected gift is always appreciated.

We use my mum to look after our children, especially when we run the Ultimate 48-Hour Author Retreats and she diarises all of my events and travel in her planner, even though she works full time herself; so we know she's not available during the weeks. When we do our Friday, Saturday, Sunday retreat, she picks up the kids from care and school on Friday after work and then hangs out at our house for the whole weekend. We then come back home on the Sunday afternoon and take over. We leave her a couple of hundred dollars to do stuff with the kids so she doesn't have to be financially strained and they have an awesome bonding time. This is a great bonding time for grandparents and children, you just have to realise that some grandparents of course feel like it's a chore to look after their grandchildren and other grandparents absolutely thrive on it and absolutely love it. They know these children will only be this little for a short period of time and they cherish that time. Also grandparents are a lot more patient and the children get to learn and experience from a different perspective and people who are obviously older and wiser.

If we look at the childcare centres, as I said earlier we did have the ad hoc ability to be more flexible in the early days. As I suggested before, the best days for childcare are Tuesdays, Wednesdays and Thursdays as this is prime time for your business.

Most childcare centres will charge you even if the child is not there, or if it's a public holiday. This is why I recommend Tuesday, Wednesday and Thursday, because Mondays do have a lot of public holidays and you can get charged over and over throughout the year when perhaps your child is not going to care and utilising the centre.

You may be eligible for quite a big rebate or childcare benefit, which would make the costs of childcare a lot easier and cheaper. Be aware that as you earn more through your empire and your business, you will need to pay closer attention to the fees as the rebates reduce. Of course at that point in time you won't need as much of that help. I always say even if you don't think you can afford childcare right now, do ensure that you work towards that because it's just going to give you so much focus and ability to really separate home life from business life.

I want to give you a big warning here about school holidays. Usually, if your children are school age, every ten weeks they generally will have a two-week school holiday. If you're in Australia there's obviously the long summer holidays as well. I'm going to point out the two-week ones can be a big, big distraction and entrepreneurial parents can lose momentum in their business if they choose to take time off during every school holiday. I've found this on many occasions and then when you lose two weeks of momentum, generally it can take you up to four weeks to get it back and for you to feel back on track.

There are school holiday programs in those times and we now send our children during the term holidays, as we tend to take most of the summer off and not put them into those types of programs. During the two-week school holidays we still send them again on Tuesday, Wednesday and Thursday so we can have the time to focus. We enjoy lots of activities on the other four days and Stuart and myself swap time for entertaining the kids during the school holidays.

If your partner works full time, remember that you will need to work around them. Work when they're home, you might need to put in time in the evenings and weekends, that's certainly what I did in the first few years of business. I used to work every single weekend and almost every single night. There was no TV, there was no other switch off entertainment, because I was so focused and determined to build a viable and successful business.

Some sacrifices do need to be made in the early days when you're working around a roster, when you have got the responsibility of having a day job. I was still in my day job for the first 13 months of my business and during the lunch break in my day job I would sit there and do some stuff on my business while others were on Facebook or chatting. It was my own personal time while I ate and I just found every spare moment that I could do it and it certainly turned out to be worth it.

If you have no parents around or you feel guilty using your parents to babysit and look after your children, then see if you can find others who you can swap baby sitting with. You will babysit for them on this night and they reciprocate. You can even create a little network of entrepreneurial parents to swap with and design a schedule of when things will happen for you and for them that might remove the guilt.

You'll be able to sense which parent, grandparent or auntie enjoy it and love it by the energy of how they say yes. The most important thing is to ask for help.

Don't be scared about saying 'I need help' and 'I need to do this' because once you are experiencing success, you will win over your tribe and they will be wanting to know everything that you are doing. At the end of the day the whole family benefits as you will be able to give back more to the people who have helped you.

If childcare is too expensive and you just can't see how you can financially make it viable for yourself, then you may need to juggle things and it's all about how you do it when your back's up against the wall. You can do the work to make the business financially viable so that you can work toward outsourcing the care.

Ultimately you want to be getting the revenue up in your business so that you can outsource the things that you don't love doing. Not to say that caring for your children is not something that you would love to do full time, however you need that separation from being a parent to being a business owner, so that you can focus and progress your business a lot faster.

Multitasking requires four times the amount of time to complete say four tasks than it would be if you did one after the other after the other. I know when I'm away from home and travelling, I get a lot more productive and a lot more done, because I'm completely on my own. Right now I'm writing this from New York City, I'm here for five nights and I have lots of times when I can just do an hours work and feel like I've achieved so much and been so productive so that when I do meet up with my family I can be 100% there for them and enjoy the time that we'll be spending together.

Make some time also to work on your business or if you do your business trips, utilise that time in hotels when it's quiet to make it actually productive and effective.

Let's link this to building your business empire:

1. Childcare will support you in achieving your business goals and giving you time to focus.
2. Your child will thrive and learn from others and build on their social skills.
3. Your child will learn from experts so they have a great start to their school life.

> "Sometimes the only answer people are looking for when they ask for help is that they won't have to face the problem alone."
>   Mark Amend

They say it takes a village to raise a child. Well, let me tell you, there were times when I wish we had that village at our disposal. There were times when it was hard and I was feeling like I was going to break. I think we all go through these thoughts with our first child, as there just isn't any off switch.

When I first started thinking about childcare for Juddy (our first) it was me who kept coming up with all the excuses as to why I didn't want him to start care. It was MY belief that I was a bad parent for not being able to look after him – simple as that. Surprisingly enough, I had these same feelings pop up a year or so later when we decided to get a house cleaner. In my head I was thinking, 'What, I can't even keep my house clean and tidy?'

Now, I can't imagine not having childcare for Xara (the older two are in school) and our cleaner has been with us for years. I now realise that the more support you can get, the more time you have to not only do the things that you love, but you can do more of the things that bring in the income. Also it is a money mindset challenge that a lot of business owners have to go through. Look at it this way, the cleaner as the first example. Instead of doing two hours a week cleaning (which is a $20 per hour task) you can use that time to consult a client, write a sales letter or get to a networking event. All of these things have the potential to earn a lot more than $20 per hour.

In Australia, childcare costs are at an all time high and many families choose not to send their kids to care, as the amount that they spend on care is sometimes more than they earn in their job. Not being flippant here but if this is the case for you, it is time that you start investigating how you can start to earn more whether it is doing a part-time business or increasing your value to either your employer or adding an additional income stream to your business.

In our case it wasn't the cost to send Judd, and then obviously our second child Mika, it was to give us the time freedom to allow me to work undistracted in the business three full days a week after I left my employed positions. Before I had left work and came into the business, we were able to find a childcare centre that were able to accommodate having Judd in care on alternate days as I had a very stable roster but different days off a week.

This was all working well for a while with Natasa planning her clients and business activities around my roster until the childcare centre decided that they wanted Judd in fixed days which we didn't want to do as we didn't want him in care when I was able to look after him. Anyway, without getting bogged down in the finer details, and possibly due to me not remembering all of the dates and times, we were able to make childcare work for us.

It was important for us to have this 'cut out' as we don't have a big family so the only person who would look after our kids even to this day was Natasa's mum. My dad is a great entertainer and loves spending time with them but he has never been one to offer to take them off our hands when they were little for a night as apparently 'nappies' aren't his forte.

Having our children happy and safe in care has satisfied my needs for my children's wellbeing while allowing me the space to become involved in more and more parts of our business. As much as you can try your hardest to 'work around your kids' when they are home with you, it is near impossible to take client calls, attend meetings and have the focus that is needed to achieve outstanding results.

At the time of writing this, mid 2017, my week is structured like this: Judd (grade 3) and Mika (prep) at school five days per week and Xara in childcare Tues, Wed and Thursday. Monday is time together for Xara and me, so after drop off we get to spend time without her older brother and sister hogging my attention. The days she is in care are the days I cram most of my work into, especially the client phone calls, meetings and mentoring calls. Friday Xara gets to spend the day with Natasa alone or with both of us if I have been able to finish up my week on Thursday night. We don't work weekends and spend them together either enjoying activities locally or taking trips, or mini-holidays as we call them, within an hour or so of home.

Childcare is great for them to socialize with other kids too. We tend to live a very isolated life and around where we have lived there have been very few kids of similar ages. They get taught new things and get prepared for their next adventure of school but most of all, we don't feel like we are doing the wrong thing by them simply having them around but ignoring them. Quality time over quantity time should be the priority all day, every day.

Secret Men's Only Section

Here are some great ways for you men to make the most of your kid's childcare and school experiences:

1. Try to be the regular drop off and pick up if you can work it into your schedules. The carers, teachers and mums swoon at a dad taking on this role.

2. Use the time to bond privately with your kids – take them to a park on the way home quickly or get them off for a quick ice-cream on the down low.

3. There is nothing better than having them excitedly sharing their day with you in the car on the way home before the distractions of home make them forget.

4. Find a local park or nature reserve close to their childcare or school and spend 30 minutes there before you start your day as a great excuse to stay active and reconnect with nature.

5. Get to know your child's carers and teacher's first name and be friendly at all times. You never know when your good relationship with them may come in handy.

Chapter 4
Day Job to Entrepreneur

HERS ♀

> "Entrepreneurship is living a few years of your life like most people won't so that you can spend the rest of your life like most people can't."
>
> Unknown

We weren't ready. Stuart was given an ultimatum from his day job to move locations. He was already out of the house for about ten and a half hours every single day and now we were faced with the decision where he would be out of the house going to and from work, taking it to a total of 12 hours per day, five days per week.

This was a time just before Christmas and he was about to get super busy at his day job. When he was given this ultimatum they said to him: either you move to the different location or there's no job here for you. We decided to take the leap. We didn't know how this was going to be, we didn't feel we were going to be safe, all we knew was that we needed to take that leap and give it a go. Travelling an extra two hours in a day to a location so far away from home was just not an option. So I said to him, just quit. And so he did a few days later.

I believe that the universe rewards those who bravely make a decision without knowing what's on the other side because in the following two and a half months, we generated two years worth of his salary in sales through the business.

When you can transition out of your day job, which is most entrepreneurs' dream, you will be able to have more time to focus on building your empire. You will be empowered that you're driving your own bus and that your income potential is limitless.

Ultimately you embark on the best ride of your life – one not for the faint at heart.

As I said, the ultimate dream of a small business owner is to make this transition but most of them never do or they do for a short period of time and then return to a day job, which is an entrepreneur's biggest nightmare.

Transitioning out of a day job can be super scary. You realise that you alone will be responsible fully for your livelihood and the livelihood of your family, especially if you have young children.

You will be stuck and reliant on individuals/clients making the decision to come on board with you or not. You'll never know what's around the corner. You'll just have to have as much faith as possible. They say that when you're an employee, you don't need faith, but when you're an entrepreneur you absolutely need faith. Often you will have those times when you feel like your business is imploding, not knowing where your next client's going to come from and those times of uncertainty can start to bring up that fear of, 'Oh my god, am I going to have to get a job if this situation does not change?'

Making a successful transition from a day job into your business is about having the confidence in your own abilities to take the leap and keep your head above water in those uncertain times of entrepreneurship. It truly is a rollercoaster. You'll have times when you'll feel like you're falling apart and others when you're on top of the world feeling invincible. The highs can be super high and the lows super low.

How do you make this transition successfully? Let's go through some of the things that we have used in our life that made me fully transition out of my day job within the first 13 months of starting the business and then Stuart transitioned out when the business was two and a half years old.

1. How do you know when you're ready? I myself am not a huge risk taker. I know a lot of people who have quit their corporate jobs and have said, 'When my back is

up against the wall I will have to make this business work' and they have left a six-figure job and ventured out completely on their own.

Then there are people who can't let go and they're really low risk takers and they just don't give themselves enough time to work on their business properly. Myself, I'm a moderate risk taker. I had a set income goal for the business before I called it quits on my day job.

My goal was to double my day job income. This was about $500 a week and my goal was to be hitting $1,000 a week for a few months consistently. Some weeks or months would have been higher or lower, but if I divided that over say a 12-week period, that I was on average making $1,000 per week. That was my sign that I was ready and confident enough to walk into my day job and hand in my resignation, which happened during my maternity leave with Mika.

The way we looked at Stuart's situation when he quit his day job, a total surprise when he was given the ultimatum, we had a similar goal. The business was consistent at the time; it needed to be bringing in at least $2,000 per week for Stuart to be able to quit his day job over a three-month period.

Even though he quit and we hadn't done the numbers at the time, I had documented everything, so when he did quit I actually had a look at how we were performing over the previous 12 weeks and we were bringing in $2,000 per week. This was a sign that it was the right time, even though we had planned to do it three months later.

So, set an income goal that you want your business to be generating for you to feel confident enough that you will be okay if you left your day job. The second thing to decide is over how long a period do you need to be making that to feel confident that you can sustain this on your own?

2. There will be moments that you wish you were back into a secure day job. How do you handle those moments? I always say, once we have taken that leap and we have transitioned out of our day job, yes, absolutely it's going to be scary, there are going to be times where we are going to feel like things are going backwards, we're losing clients, that we're not moving forward and start to get huge amounts of fear come up to us.

    The point is to just remember, if you got your business to a certain level of success and income, obviously you did certain things to make that happen. What were all of those things that you were doing when you were getting your clients? What kind of marketing activities? Where did you go? Who were the people you spoke to? I always say to people, usually **when things stop working it's because you have stopped doing what you know works.**

I often ask people the ultimate coaching question. I was given this back in my first few days of studying to become a coach. When things stop working towards achievement of your goal, ask yourself this question:

What are you pretending to not know that if you were to know it, it would enable you to make the change easily and effortlessly even more right now?

Many will answer: 'I don't know, I'm not pretending, I have no idea'. Right? But usually the answer is that you have started to pretend that you don't know that you need to hustle, to get out there, to go out networking, to talk to people, to generate interest around your offer, to have a call to action, to set up joint ventures, to be on social media, to add value, to send emails to your database.

Usually people get paralysed with fear, so what they pretend not to know is that they need to have that consistent intention to turn up and promote themselves and all the things that go with running a successful business. But if you've stopped getting clients or clients finish up and others are not signing up, it's also because you're maybe not vibrating at a level that's creating attraction towards your business. You've lost a bit of self-confidence and to bring all of that back up, you need to get the energy going, the motion going. As they say, motion creates emotion. It will generate momentum and start to bring positive things towards you.

I know when I go quiet within myself, everything around me goes quiet. When I get out there and I'm with people and I'm talking, hustling, having the calls to action, doing my sales and marketing, things roll forward. The momentum takes me forward and I achieve results out of this world. Next time you slow down, please ask yourself that ultimate coaching question and see what is it that you have stopped doing that you know works.

Remember you can always go back to a day job if things really get desperate. Even if it's something part-time to bring the cash flow in so that you can pay your core bills to keep your roof above your head and put food on the table. I know it's super scary, because you could be a single parent, you could be responsible for 1-3 children that are very young, so it is a big, big responsibility that we choose to lead forward with when it comes to not having anyone to seek secure employment.

I still can't believe it's been five years on our own and we're okay. It's great if you can have a support system and a buddy like I have my Stuart who I can talk to about my fears when they come up. I have an awesome friend who said it quite simply. Her name is Rosemary McCallum. She said no matter what, I can always clean houses. Anyone can clean houses and there's always demand for a job like that and it's reasonably well paid. She always says I can go do that if things get super desperate.

I love that it makes it seem like it's possible for anyone. There are plenty of jobs where you can add value to other people if you had to. But of course I want you to be able to sustain your business and keep it growing and evolving to the next levels as you evolve on this journey as well.

Transitioning out of a day job can be scary but there's always ways to go around it or recover if things don't go well. If you're scared, just remember the universe rewards those who are courageous. Remember, say yes and then work out the 'how'. When was the last time that you were ready to do anything when there was a significant change in your life? You were probably pushed into making a decision when you weren't ready, because you had to do that and then things did work out.

There's another saying that goes something like this: The best time to start something is when you're not ready!

For those of you who might have had to go back to a day job and you have that sense of failure that you didn't make it on your own, it's okay to admit that you've got to do what you've got to do. You've got to look after yourself, you must survive and it's not failing, so long as you're looking after you and your family, that's not failure, that's you succeeding on your journey and this is just a moment in time.

Out of moments where you've had the failure that seems to be the biggest deal, are also the biggest learnings that you'll probably be teaching people about who will be facing the same situations in the future. In my public speaking, I often talk about my sad moments, moments I've cried and moments I've just been in the biggest state of desperation, because they're the ones where I found the best gold nugget lessons.

When temptation strikes to look into going back to a day job, just do what you know works to grow your business. It's easy to give into temptation, just throw the towel in and not have your business hanging over your head. In these times I want you to remember how much you love those moments when you are going well and you are feeling empowered and you know if you've done it once before you can do it again.

As your journey throughout the business builds year after year, you will know that there are seasons. There will be springs, summers, autumns and winters but always come back to your *why*. Know what your *why* is and keep revisiting that and know that there's always another option if you need to take it.

Let's link this up to building your business empire:

1. The universe rewards those who take the leap. You will work it out when your back is up against the wall.
2. Remember there are lots of options should you need to generate more cash.
3. Revisit your why when temptation strikes to want to return to a day job.

> "97% of the people who quit too soon are employed by the 3% who never gave up."
> Unknown

HIS

When I think back to where it all began, it seems like a lifetime ago. Life as we know it now simply didn't exist, nor could even the thought of it. When I lost the business, and I call it a business very loosely as even though I had 'bought in' and had some small authority to make decisions, the Specsavers powerbrokers controlled 90% of the decisions. Up until then, I had worked as an employee of OPSM, Australia's leading spectacle retailer, for 12 years beginning as an apprentice optical technician and ending up managing their largest Victorian stores. Post losing the Specsavers, I managed Melbourne International Airport Departures, Cash Converters and then moved into BigBox retail management at Barbeques Galore.

For 15 years I had to start when they wanted me to, knock off when they said and ask permission to take personal days and annual leave. When you work for 'the man' every decision you make, even when it seems you have the authority to do things your way, is dictated by the higher chain of command. There is a saying I love, 'If you work hard for 40 hours a week as a employee, you might be lucky enough to be promoted to manager and then work really hard for 60 hours a week for very little more'.

I am sure Natasa will have shared her stories about how she went about transitioning from part-time management work post-baby number one so as this needs to give both sides of things, this is what it looked like from my perspective.

I had really messed up (we look at things quite differently these days) so I was doing everything I could to bring in a salary and bonuses, with my management roles, while Natasa was throwing herself in to life coaching. As soon as I arrived home from work I would cook us dinner and then take over the care of Judd for his night time routine and Natasa would leave me and go downstairs into her 'woman cave' (the downstairs office) and start either furthering her study, coaching clients one-on-one, or working on her business. It was lonely, and I felt very left out of the new life she was trying to create for us.

Natasa made it clear that she no longer felt that she could rely on anyone else (me) to support her so she needed to make a go of it herself. So I shouldered as much of the home duties as I could with the 50 hours I was away from home with work.

I never doubted that success would come for Natasa, I had seen her results at all of the management positions she had held over the years but seeing only $7,000 come in through the business in the first year was tough especially seeing the amount of work she was putting in.

Things pretty much stayed the same for a bit over two years until things started to change. Her first book proved the catalyst for her own personal growth and subsequent business growth. The money started to come in on the back of her fully booked coaching business plus her licensing Ultimate Weight Loss and signing on other coaches who would use her systems and IP.

With her running out of hours, as there was only so much she could do with Judd, even though he was in care a few days a week, working around my roster was a challenge.

It wasn't until my then company Barbeques Galore decided they wanted to initiate a managers swap, meaning all managers had to move to a different store at random, which meant that I would have to spend an extra two hours per day away from home, that Natasa and I made the decision that I would resign and join her full time in the business. We weren't 100% ready for this to happen as the licensing had only just started and we didn't have the security that we would've liked to but we made a leap of faith that everything would work out in the end.

It did and in the next 30 days we made as much in income as I would've in 12 months wages at my job and the rest is history.

I must admit, I thought this business stuff would come easily but I was wrong. I had almost become institutionalized with my employee mindset and struggled for the first 12 months to understand what it meant to own and run a business that needed so many different parts managed to be a success.

Self motivation shouldn't have been that hard with what I had put our family through losing the security and safety of the optical business those few short years ago yet for some reason, as things were starting to tick along nicely, I took things easy and did what I now know was the bare minimum that needed to be done and I lapped up the 'stay at home dad' role.

This is still in my opinion the number one reason why most solopreneur and small first time businesses fail, not through lack of talent or a great offering, but the discipline and structures that are required to keep you motivated and to this day it is still a work in progress.

A lot of people say to me they could never work with their partner and are amazed that we seem to make it work. We compliment each other with different skill sets and now that we have such defined roles within our business and we outsource things that we don't enjoy to virtual assistants and consultants, we run the business like a well-oiled machine.

Secret Men's Only Section

Here are some tips if you ever end up working with your partner:

1. She is never wrong, or if she is, you have nothing to gain by proving it.
2. Don't be surprised if you have differences of opinions on the way you do things within the business. Just remember, hers are always best.
3. If there is something that needs to change, (and you know hand on heart that it is best for your business) change them and show her an example of how it has improved operations – and then make it seem like it was her idea.
4. Be the rock that she needs you to be. Women are more emotional than men and can take things personally if things aren't going well. Assure her that things will be okay and that together you are stronger.
5. Although there are a few tongue-in-cheek tips here, remember this one above all else. Make sure you have very defined roles within your business, this way you can operate as a separate identity when you need and it doesn't become an employee-employer relationship which will end badly very quickly.

Chapter 5
From Fear to Faith

HERS

"The only known cure for Fear is Faith."
Lena Kellogg Sadler

Fear is the best tracking device you will have on your entrepreneurial parenting journey. Your dream life lives on the other side of fear. It's something that you will experience time and time again. I believe not one person in this world is immune to fear, even if you're the most successful billionaire out there.

When you go through fear and you push through, the feeling is absolutely amazing. I'm sure you can think of a time when you faced the fear and did it anyway. Usually when you start to get those sick feelings in your stomach, you should go and move forward, because this is you being challenged by the boundary that you have put within your own reality.

Fear comes up from our little critter brain. Fear comes up because our critter brain believes if we do something that we haven't done before, it means death. It is that prehistoric brain that we still have that only knows survival or death.

Often we manifest a lot of subconscious self-sabotage if we're scared of doing something, which is a whole lot more reason to do it. In today's world there aren't too many things that we should fear in order to succeed and achieve the results that we want. When you expand your comfort zone, you start to see yourself getting bigger and better results as you move through different stages and you continue to evolve your business and yourself.

Stepping past fear means getting to the next level of income, attracting and connecting with people that you never had the opportunity to before.

Did you know that fear and faith live in the opposite sides of the brain? This is a really cool tip that I learnt very early in my business and personal development journey. I learnt that if you focus on faith, you cannot focus on fear at the same time. It's impossible. Whenever I get scared or fearful of what's going to happen and I start having those 'what if' moments in my head, I start to focus on faith, being grateful and appreciative.

Focusing on gratitude, appreciation and writing it out as well as focusing on having that faith that things will work out, one way or another; it's going to dissipate and make the fear go away. If you stay stuck in fear, you will stay stuck in life and business. It will feel like you are stuck in a groundhog day without progress, without growth, you'll end up having a mediocre life that is boring with less opportunities. Ultimately you will pass this on as a strategy that your children will play out later on in their life, because they're constantly observing what risks, challenges and opportunities you are saying yes to and they're watching a lot more through your behaviour than the things that you say.

FEAR has been said to stand for False Expectations Appearing Real. And one thing to realise is that as human beings, we're only born with two primal fears: the fear of falling and the fear of loud noises. Every other fear is learnt along the way after birth. Many books have been written on this, one of my favourites is from Susan Jeffers, *Feel the Fear and Do It Anyway*.

In this chapter I want to unpack for you the top three fears for entrepreneurial parents and how to live and deal with them as they rear their ugly heads from time to time and continue to do so.

The number one fear for entrepreneurs and entrepreneurial parents is ***the fear of going back to a day job***. This is one that will come up a lot more for you in the early days especially 0–2 years in the business. Things will go up and down and you won't be sure if there's any consistency in your business. What I always say to people is do what you know works, because usually when you get scared and things have slowed down, it's usually because you have stopped doing what you know works. What you need to do is step up your actions, increase your activities, get out there a lot more, do more marketing, talk to more people, collaborate with more people and always know that you have an option. Ultimately if you have to, go back to a day job. You can go back and generally find some kind of employment that's going to pay the bills.

I've had many moments where I felt like the business wasn't flowing, even at a 7-figure level. Sometimes it can feel like everything around you has stopped working or people aren't coming and you have stopped getting enquiries. You can go through times when you are getting way more 'no's' than 'yes's'. You can have real moments of drought and this can be scary, but the thing to remember is that you need to keep putting one foot in front of the other and at the end of the day know that courage is the ability to get up the next day and say, 'I will do it all again.'

That fear of going back to a day job does dissipate and becomes less on your mind as you become more successful. You recognise what this is as it comes up and in those moments this is a sign and a time for you to step it up even more and do some wonderful work and find new connections. This will create new and bigger momentum around your business. Building momentum and having opportunities lined up is what's going to make that fear go away.

The second fear that entrepreneurial parents have is the *fear of missing out on time with children*, especially if the children are little. I have experienced that from time to time. I still think about whether I have missed out on anything when I'm interstate or overseas on business. But I know that I'm modelling different strengths and traits to Stuart, which means that my children are going to learn different things about nurturing through him and more of the entrepreneurial side of things from me.

What I know in my heart is that my children and your children will love us no matter what. I always focus on quality time over quantity time and being present with them. One thing that we do in our family is to book one-on-one dates with our kids. Every child's different; he or she has different interests, especially at different ages. Ours are three years apart; from one, two and three and I always ask them what they want to do for their date. One of them always chooses to go to the movies, the other one likes to do girly things and the baby just wants to be with me. Whatever it is that they want to do, I give them that choice and that way we can create really special moments one-on-one with them.

Talk to them regularly even if you feel you are getting nowhere. What answer did you get the last time you asked: How is school? I bet it was, 'Good!' I think that's the most annoying answer ever. I have learnt since that there are other questions you can ask like: What was the most exciting thing about today? What's the best thing that happened today? Those are some great quality questions, being open ended versus the closed ended 'How was school today?'

Sometimes when I'm on planes I write letters to them and I know that they're not going to read some of that stuff when they're little, but I write to them in the form of a journal and I know that one day they will pick it up and they'll read it and find wonderful meaning and connection through the writing.

Number three fear of being an entrepreneurial parent is the *fear of being found out*. We call this the Impostor Syndrome, which lives inside all of us. You can see this fear being played out when people ask these questions of themselves: Am I good enough? Do I know enough? Who am I to write or talk about this topic? I always say, Who are you not to? Who is going to find you out and what are they going to find out about you? Seriously. So long as you have integrity behind what you're doing, you have nothing to worry about.

As long as you're teaching and showing people things that you have achieved with integrity and when you put your head on the pillow at night you know you have done the right thing to the best of your knowledge, you have no reason to feel like an impostor.

In Australia we have what we call the Tall Poppy syndrome and people are too scared to get cut down if they start rising above others. It's all 'false expectations appearing real' as we said earlier. If you just back yourself you'd find that you will have a lot more support than people giving you flack. Do it anyway, because those people who love you and follow you will give you more encouraging comments and statements and people who are not on your wavelength tend to stay out of the way and un-friend you on Facebook if they are not that into you.

From moment to moment yes, we are going to get someone who makes you feel like a fraud or challenges your integrity, but the most important thing, the person you need to be true to is yourself, because deep down if you know you're doing the right thing, there's nothing to worry about. If you know that you're being dodgy or being scammy, then certainly this is going to start being reflected in your world. I can tell you, 99.9% of my journey in the last seven years of business, I've heard way more positive things than the 0.01% of negative things that I may have come across of someone trying to tear me down.

It's totally worth you just owning what you stand for.

When other people question your integrity, as I said very rarely on a couple of occasions that has happened to me, it's a sign that this is important to you. When I felt bad about my integrity being questioned, someone said to me it was because it's one of my top values. And if it's important to you and if this is a challenge, this is usually a challenge that the universe is sending you and asking you that question – Are you worthy of your success? Will you keep going? Even in spite of this particular situation or whatever this person has said or done?

People often ask me how do I deal with the want of the stability of a day job? It just seems so much easier not to take all that responsibility. It can be quite hard. When you feel like you just want to throw in the towel and go get a job, because you can just go and do your eight hours and then come back home, I want you to revisit your WHY.

Your why should be written out: WHY you started the business and what will it create for your life. When you revisit your why, make sure it also includes the contribution that it will be making in this world. When you look at that, you have a greater responsibility to make your business a success over just going and serving at an employee level.

If you start feeling distant from your kids, because you do go away often for business, just remember that making the time that you have with them great quality time, being present, being there, being interested, being engaged, it's really important. If you start feeling distant from your kids, it could be the way you are using the time you're spending with them and that you may not be connecting. If you're being distracted by devices that we have today – mobile, computers – then switch them off at least one day out of a week. Saturday is usually the best day to get off the Internet, get off Facebook, stop checking emails and connect with your family.

Let's link this up to building your business empire:

1. Fear is here to stay. Learn to notice it and use it to your advantage as a tracking device.
2. Acting with integrity will always protect you from feeling like an impostor.
3. Your kids will benefit from you stretching your comfort zone, as they will do the same as they grow.

> "Fear occupies the same space and Faith. And there's only room for one."
>   Brian Logue

I am sure that Natasa has taken you through the fears that would arise for entrepreneurs and parents in her chapter and most likely they will be from the woman's perspective. In saying that, the question I ponder is, are fears the same for all of us? Fears are really just a conditioning of our upbringing, as we aren't born with fears except the fear of loud noises and the fear of falling. Why do some people have a fear of heights, and others a fear of bugs? Some fears are irrational, like my own fear of spiders yet I can hold a four metre long snake around my neck without blinking. Other fears are rational or easier to understand.

If you have been attacked while walking through an underground car park, it is understandable that each time you are in that situation that fear returns. Does it mean that you are more at risk than anyone else? No, yet the fear is more real as it is based on an actual event that took place.

The fears that hold us back the most, in my opinion, are the fears of things that we don't even know. Many people fear success even though they have never experienced it before yet do anything they can to sabotage their chances of it. They fear what their friends will think, they fear what impact it will have on their family lives and their own time. In other words, they fear what 'might' happen and never actually live that life to see if their fears are founded.

Now don't get me wrong, I am not advising not to think of the potential consequences of your decisions and actions. What I am stressing is the importance of not letting an irrational fear hold you back from doing what you know you want to do. We took a risk when I decided to resign from my management position from Barbeques Galore as we didn't know if we could make a real success of our licensing program that we had just launched but we didn't let the fear of failure stop us from making what we knew was the right decision.

Michael Jordan, arguably the world's greatest basketball player, said, "You will never miss any of the shots that you don't take but you will never make any of them and win a game either".

The most common fear that I hear from parents who are building their own business that will hopefully turn into their own empire is, 'What if I get too busy that my children miss out on having their mum/dad around?' The simple answer is you are the only one who controls how busy you become, period! No one will make you take on that extra client or work every weekend but you. And so what if you do? Wouldn't being busy be a wonderful thing? That way you can outsource all of your admin, get a team of helpers and do only the things in your business that bring you joy and fulfilment.

The best gift you can give your kids is the gift of independence and quality, happy family time. It doesn't mean you need to be in their face 24/7, it is much more important to be 100% present when you are with them than 25% engaged and being on your phone or computer with them all of the time. Show them that there is more than a 9-5 existence working hard for someone else to achieve their dreams at the expense of sacrificing yours.

The other fear that I hear a lot is, 'What will others think of me?' Without being flippant, but what others think of you is none of your business! Tall poppy syndrome will always exist and it happens for two reasons. Firstly, it is those who are jealous of your success and who are recognizing their own shortcomings and lack of courage who try to bring you down. Secondly, it happens that people want to keep you where you are, as they can only relate to those who have a similar income and belief system to them.

There are a lot of people from my past who I can no longer relate to, as our beliefs and way we chose to live our lives are so completely different. It doesn't mean that I judge the way they live their lives, it simply is different to how I live mine. I still consider them friends but in the big book of life, the part they played was for a few chapters only, rather than a starring role.

Being a parent is a role that I would not swap for any other in this world. Whether I had a job and worked for someone else, or have the business that I have today, my life is more complete with them in my life. Having a flourishing business, that started from one of my darkest moments shows that whatever stage you are at in your life, the best is yet to come if you have a big enough reason.

Secret Men's Only Section

So you got to the end, the very end. If this were life, it would be the same as you meeting your maker. But thankfully, it isn't and you have your entire life in front of you. Here are my five best tips I can give you to live a life filled with love, success and gratitude:

1. Life is best lived sharing it with others. Love with every part of you, give freely, be generous with your time and make other peoples life richer for having you be part of it.

2. Stop saying you can't and start saying how can I? I can guarantee that on your deathbed you will never regret that kiss you stole, that trip you took or that business you started in your mum's garage. You will regret those things you never did that you wished you had the courage to do.

3. You will f#$k up at some stage in your life. Whatever you do, do not let that moment define the rest of your life or who you are as a person. From the greatest tragedy, the greatest accomplishment can rise.

4. You have to have faith. Now, whatever faith means to you is okay by me. If that is your God, The Universe, or any other deity, have faith in yourself that you are destined for a magnificent life.

5. Be kind – The simplest yet seemingly hardest thing for the world to be to each other. It starts with YOU. Be kind and be a beacon of hope for all others.

Chapter 6
Discovering Wealth Through Values

HERS

> "It's not our job as parents to try and fix our children, but rather to observe their values, love them, and communicate within their value system. If children are inspired by what they do, they'll not only excel at it, they'll be training themselves to do what they love."
>
> Dr John Demartini

Stuart used to get annoyed with me when I did business stuff on holidays and I would get frustrated when he didn't. That was all until we learned about our value system, why we do the things that we do and why we prioritise different things that we each do. When you understand your value system and your partner's and then your children's in due course, you will fully understand what is important to others. Having that awareness will reduce conflict and frustration in times when you feel it coming up for you, you'll understand and actually be able to catch yourself and stop and think about why that person is behaving the way they are.

Values often give us answers to other people's behaviours. What is it that they prefer and what is it that we prefer? As you get to understand what each person in your family values you will end up thriving as a family and you will understand yourself and others so much more.

Conflict generally comes from clashing values. When people have clashing values, fights will start to erupt, others will start being blamed, the family will suffer, there will be disconnection and ultimately resentment and rejection can eventuate.

Values are things, people, actions and situations we give most preference to. Most people think values are personality traits, like integrity, honesty, and freedom. After I learnt from Dr John Demartini through his Values Determination Process, I started to understand that values were something different. He describes it in a way that makes total sense to how I've started to see them. It is about figuring out what are the things we talk about, spend money on the most of all, who do we surround ourselves with. It is what our internal dialogue is mostly about, as well as external dialogue and a series of other things that he goes through.

This is where our true values lie. About 6-7 months into my business, I discovered Dr John Demartini. I admire him and I've read all his books. I completed his 13 questions to see what the common 5-6 answers are that help you determine what your values are.

I'm sure if you looked him up and looked up the value determination process you'd be able to discover how to do it by yourself. My top three at the time came out to be 'education of self and others', 'business' and 'money'.

My family was not near the top of my values. When I did the same test on my husband, we found out that his top three were family, home and then obviously the business. We had our values in total reverse order. In other assessments I've found that I am driven by challenge and Stuart is driven by lifestyle.

Through my challenge, I get to grow the business and achieve all of my goals and keep stretching out of my comfort zone, which ultimately provides the resources to be able to afford the lifestyle, whereas Stuart is the opposite. He would nurture the family and do the lifestyle stuff first and then he'll take care of business second.

We are a perfect match because we don't have a clash. Our values are actually complementary to each other. I highly recommend that you look up the values determination process from Dr John Demartini and then do it for yourself. Then do it for yourself every 6–12 months to see if your values have shifted over a period of time. Values do change as we have defining moments in our lives and they do change as we go through different seasons in our lives. Our defining moment was when Stuart lost the Specsavers business. If this came up seven years prior to that, I would say family and lifestyle would have been one of my top two values, whereas that moment shifted the trajectory of my life, thus the alignment of where the values lied.

Here is where I believe some of the problems occur with mumpreneurs. They prioritise family when their wish and desire is to actually have a successful business that is financially viable and supports their family, therefore gives them a flexible lifestyle. However, if the top value is actually family and spending time with your family, then you are going to drop everything before you actually do the business stuff.

Unfortunately in the first one to three years of a fresh new start-up there's a lot of infrastructure that needs to be set up and things to be learnt. You're totally at that frontal lobe learning, you don't have enough space in your brain to fit in everything to find that perfect balance. To get the business to a viable point in those early years, the top few values have to be based around business, self-development and money. Otherwise you're going to prioritise everything that you're going to do with your family first.

Not to say if someone was sick or there was an emergency that you wouldn't drop everything to do that, but often people will do their housework instead of building their business. I had to completely remove housework. I used to be a very obsessive compulsive person when it comes to cleaning, when it comes to tidying things up and being very organised and I'd be almost like my husband said, I was that man from Sleeping with the Enemy. I would turn everything to face front in the pantry and all that sort of stuff before we had kids. As we had kids we started to be messier and we started to ... no not messier, the kids just take priority. We'd rather spend more time with them than keep the house like it was a display home.

I really dropped the ball when it came to housework when the business started, because I thought I needed as much time as possible to learn everything I needed to learn, to implement, to go out networking and really put in that obsessed type of approach towards building the business.

In my mind I needed to get it to a certain point before I could allow myself the luxury of having time to just chill out and go on holidays. Actually that was the longest period of time we hadn't even gone on holidays. For anyone who knows me, they know that I go on holidays pretty much every three months – I go somewhere.

During that period I think we went about 18 months to two years without a holiday. I also used to work through every single weekend, because that was my opportunity whilst Stuart was in his day job to actually run the business and to catch up on stuff when I wasn't being distracted by children.

This chapter is all about understanding where you need to actually be and you can and have the power to realign your values and consciously go, 'This is going to be my hierarchy of values in this period of time and that will shift and evolve as I go along'. First of all you need to understand them. It's to take the values determination test, figure out where you sit at naturally and then figure out where you need to shift or what do you need to change to be able to grow your business to a certain point.

I've discovered that there's this rule of thumb of two years, that it takes two years of focused action, consistency and effort to reach that tipping point where you will move through to the other side and experience some kind of inner reward and success. I've noticed that through various things in my life when I've started something new, it was very uncomfortable, I didn't like it, it was very time consuming, whatever I needed to do to make it better.

Please don't think that just because you decide to start a business and then you're kind of dabbling for two years, that's not the two years, I'm talking about. I'm talking about two years where you make it your obsession, you're really focused, and you really get out there and do 'the do' every single day. I get up every day and just focus on the next thing that needs to be done. I certainly have my goals laid out. I have them broken down backwards to smaller chunks and then from yearly to 90 days to weekly to daily goals and daily task lists. I focus on activities that are going to get me closer to making the business financially viable, because that's ultimately how I get to help other people and vice versa. We get to keep living life on our terms.

Values are going to really be the make or break point to you building a successful business and of course the guilt. Yes, it was absolutely there in those first couple of years for me too. I have to say I did sacrifice a lot of time where I would go downstairs on weekends, I would be downstairs in the evenings when my husband and Stuart and Judd would be up there together, but deep down in my heart and soul I knew that I was doing that for the future of the rest of our lives and one of my favourite quotes is that, *'Entrepreneurs live a few years of their life like a few people won't, so they can live the rest of their lives like most people can't.'*

I have to say seven years on, the last four years we've lived life on our terms. We've travelled the world, our kids travel with us, we enjoy quality time, connecting, exploring new cultures, new languages, new worlds and still just calling the shots as we choose to.

If you do find out that your partner has identical values, then work out whom else can support filling the gaps in some of the areas that you guys don't value. I always say, you might need to live it out tough for a little while until you can start outsourcing areas or weaknesses that exist within you and your partner and ultimately your business should end up containing people who are going to have different strengths and weaknesses to support the business in areas where their strengths are.

If you don't like your partner's values that could definitely be a place where you can find yourself. Generally we tend to attract the partner that is a perfect fit for us and actually fulfils our weaknesses. I've learnt this by being coached by my mentors over the years and together with my husband and the things that often frustrate me about Stuart are actually the perfect match to my weaknesses. One of our differences is that I can be quite futuristic and think about what's going to happen in one year, five years time and sometimes I can reach moments of anxiety where I just feel worried and there's nothing to worry about, because I'm just living the future. Whereas one of Stuart's biggest strengths is to be present and in the now and how can we fix this problem now if a problem exists, rather than worrying about what will happen in the future.

So obviously it's perfect, because he can be my rock and he can make me feel calmer and more at ease just to bring me back to the present over me thinking about the future. Yet the future is also important, because I'm the visionary and I create and move us as a family towards that vision. If you determine that your values are family and you desperately want to be successful in your business, then just realise that you may just need to make some sacrifices for a period of time until you can fully live within what you prefer to value as the most important things.

It's not going to be like that all of the time. There were moments in that first couple of years where I thought, 'Oh my god, is life going to be like this? Who am I?' I used to be really social and have lots of social activities in my calendar and just do lots of entertainment driven things in my life before I had a business and now it was all study and mentoring and going to seminars and networking. I promise you, it does change, you will change, you will adjust, you will evolve and you will also clear up space in the frontal lobe of your brain and it will move back to the back and will become more second nature. Like driving a car for the first time, when you need to be concentrating and fully alert and fully aware as to what you're doing and where you're going, you will end up being able to run your business more like a confident, experienced driver as time progresses. It's just as they say, everything is awkward as it becomes easy.

How do you link this to your business?

1. Your business will thrive and grow if your values are aligned in the correct order.
2. Your wealth is hidden in your highest top two values.
3. Our partner's values complement our own values in most cases. Use that to your strength.

> "When your Values are clear, making decisions becomes easier."
> Roy E. Disney

HIS ♂

I honestly believe that where so many relationships fail is when each partner fails to understand the other one's values. Now that seems pretty easy right? I guess the first part of it is knowing what your partners values are but the second part is the hardest for many, and that is not only understanding them, but accepting and even loving them even if they are different from yours.

As we have said all along, we haven't read the other person's section of this book but I would stake my hard earned cash on the fact that Natasa will have already told the story of how we used to drive each other crazy on 'holidays'.

Now, with my two leading values – family and quality time – holidays meant one thing for me: switching off, connecting and being together without 'work' or in our case 'the business' getting in the way. In fact, I would've been happier if it wasn't mentioned once. Natasa on the other hand, spent hours on her phone or laptop either working on the business or wanting to talk 'shop'.

I used to get so resentful of this time she spent on the business and she would feel isolated that she was the 'only one' that would still focus on the business. I hated her phone and hated her laptop and at times didn't see the point of even going on holidays. She hated my perceived 'laziness' and 'disinterest' and that didn't make for some very enjoyable moments on our holidays.

So what changed? Did we change our behaviours to appease the other person? No, to this day we still operate almost the same as we did at the beginning of the business. Natasa still likes to stay connected with her community, so Facebook and Snapchat get a good working over and she still has a focus on the business. What has changed is not only my perception of the situation, but also my acceptance of the fact that by doing what she does, it brings her happiness and makes her feel secure that the business will continue to thrive.

There are 24 hours in a day and 16 of those hours as a rule you are awake and doing things. If Natasa chooses to spend two hours a day on her work, or on most days just one hour, how many of the rest of those 14 or 15 hours was I wasting being angry?

Have I suddenly started changing my behaviour on holidays? No, as I need to switch off my brain and take time out re-aligning myself so that I can give my best in the care of our family and our clients. Natasa now understands that if I don't have this time to switch off, I do not enjoy my time and she would never want that, as she knows how much I put in not only to the business, but also being the primary carer for our three kids.

In saying that, the more involved I have become in our business, and it can take some time for the second person (in this case myself) coming into something someone else (Natasa) started, the more I know the importance of keeping the wheels turning in the business. The fact that I am writing this chapter poolside at our condo where we are currently holidaying in LA will show that some things have changed, but just ever so slightly.

As a partner, we should always encourage our significant other to do things they enjoy and fulfil their needs. If they feel great after having a mani and pedi day with their girlfriends, then encourage it. It shows that you support them and you know what makes them happy. We all need as much happiness in our lives as we can get, so make sure you create the non-judgmental space for them to be their best.

A great exercise to do when you find yourself being upset at some of the things your partner does is to ask yourself why it is that you are actually angry with them. Are they doing something to deliberately upset you? Or in fact does it have nothing to do with you at all and only about themselves, and are they doing it because it makes them happy?

Then there is something even deeper that might be rearing its head from the depths of your thoughts. Let me start with a story. Years ago now, when I was in my 'day job' while I was transitioning into the business I started to have a very deep-set anger towards the 'hippy' and 'surfer' types. Whenever I saw one on the news being interviewed or simply passed one on the street I could feel my anger levels rising. I blamed their unkempt appearance, carefree attitude towards working, dirty feet etc. etc. (see my judgment here).

It wasn't until I decided to look deeper within me to find the answer as to why these actions annoyed me so much that I finally uncovered what it was. These people were not doing anything to upset me. In fact they didn't even know I existed. It was in fact my shadow self (the one that knows the truth) that wanted to have some small part of what they had. No responsibilities, connection to the earth and a carefree existence away from the pressures of a job, a business and family to look after. It was a real breakthrough.

Now if we take this back to the relationship with your partner, perhaps it could be that their behaviours and actions are getting on your nerve but you don't know why. There is some part of you that wants it too but you don't know how to make it happen. The key is to do what you love and love what you do. And if there is something that you want to do, just bring it up with your partner. Remember, as much as we might think they are at times, they aren't a mind reader!

Secret Men's Only Section

Here are some simple ways you can get to do more of what YOU want:

1. Give your partner the time and support to do what they want to do – (stay with me guys it will all make sense soon).
2. The more they get to do things that fulfil their values, the more they will accept your wants.
3. Don't be passive aggressive, nothing says insecure and needy more than a man that won't ask for what he wants (back to my mind reader point from earlier).
4. As Nike says, just do it. Nine times out of ten it isn't your partner who won't support what you want to do, it is an incorrect belief that your partner won't want you to.
5. Be nice to their mum – if their mum likes you, you are set.

Chapter 7
Six Figures Part Time

HERS

> "Change your focus from making money to serving more people. Serving more people makes the money come in."
> Robert Kiyosaki

I never started my business with an intention to build it to seven-figures. They got me at 'six-figure business – part time hours'. That was the advertising when I was looking on the Internet to understand what coaching was about. The coaching school that I decided to go for sold this idea of having a six-figure business working part-time hours. That sounded awesome to me, because I was working part-time at that time in my day job and I certainly was nowhere near six-figure income. I thought if I could do this, then we would have me being able to be a mum at home as well as provide for the things we wanted to do and have an awesome lifestyle. Six figures at the time was something that was quite enormous in my mind.

I decided I would enrol in this $15,000 course to become a life coach. I learnt since about marketing that we sell people what they want and we give them what they need. We sell to the ego and we give to the soul. In this case it was selling the dream lifestyle in order for me to take the leap and then giving me the tools I needed to get to that point.

The first couple of years couldn't be further from the lifestyle I dreamt of. To get to that six figure level took 80 hours consistently, per week. There were no way six figures, part-time hours. Looking back, even nowadays I spend a lot of time, at least full time hours, each and every week and some weeks I do more. Other times we do go on a lot of holidays. However, it did eventually get to the lifestyle that the marketing promised. It may not be the hours they promised but if I did downsize my business nowadays it would be part-time, but I did build a business that drives my dream life.

Why would you want to do that? A lot of people might say, 'Oh, I don't need six or seven figures'. Well it's really not about the seven figures, so keep reading.

If you choose to build a six- or a seven-figure business, you will end up having a lifestyle not many people have. You will be able to provide for your loved ones without stressing, without thinking about a surprise bill. You will eventually be not just able to help your family, but help many others beyond and outside of your family, because you'll be able to give back more. As you grow financially, you also grow as a person. This happens very rapidly, because this ends up being the biggest personal development journey of your life.

As you grow, you start to mingle and be introduced to other influencers, who will help lift you higher and help you to evolve and grow to the next levels of your journey.

In my first six months when I started out as a coach I had a quick realisation that this was not going to be as easy as I thought. It was actually an email that hit my inbox that had three facts it shared. Those facts were:

1. Less than 1% of coaches ever build a six-figure business.
2. 95% of coaches will spend more on their education than they will ever earn through their business.
3. 9/10 coaches will quit within the first nine months of starting.

They also warned us at our coaching school about month nine being the month most new coaches quit because they exert so much effort and energy and study and when they are not seeing things progress, they start to wonder, 'This is not my passion, it's not for me, maybe I was not cut out for this', and they end up talking themselves out of the journey and quit.

If you don't persist, take action and make your business financially viable, whether that's a six- or seven-figure level, you can end up working triple what you did in your day job for the same or less money.

When you run your own business, it's a completely different feel. You don't look at how much time you are investing or calculate an hourly rate. You look at the value that you are bringing into this world. The journey into a seven-figure business that I went through was very much unpacked in a book that I wrote called *Natasa Denman Reveals … 1000 Days to a Million Dollar Coaching Business From Home*. What this chapter will cover is the life and family challenges and sacrifices that it took to grow this business to this level and what people and support I needed to do this.

Let's tap into what happened and how it can happen for you:

1. You don't need to know how you're going to get to six or seven figures – you just need to set that intention. My first intention was, 'Hey I'd love to have that six-figure business while working part time hours'. When I started out I learnt about goal setting, vision boards and setting intentions. I love that kind of stuff, I even did it before I had become a coach and so I decided to create my new vision board. On this vision board I dreamt big and put up $100,000 per month. In the first two years I was looking at that on the board and I would say to myself: 'Why in the hell did I put $100,000 a month, because I don't even know how to get to $100,000 per year', yet I put that per month on there. As time went on, I looked at my vision board, but it was just there to the side and I would look at it and say, 'I'm just being ridiculous here, right?'

    But one day it happened. It was about 3.5 years after I started and put that on my vision board that I had my first $100,000 month. I didn't know what I didn't know to get to that point. I underwent a lot of growth and took so much action. It almost felt like, Aha this is how you do it; and it wasn't such a huge deal once I got there.

But I did get there and I thought, my goodness, this vision board stuff does work and a lot of the things were coming true so I was taking stuff off and adding other things on. Nowadays I've stretched myself even further and I've put down the million-dollar month. I've done a million dollars a year and I've had months that have been about $250,000-$275,000. My biggest was $275,000, but I'm nowhere near the million dollar month right now. That's okay, because I'm kind of going, you know what, if it happens it happens, if it doesn't I won't be disappointed. If the $100,000 month happened, then this is totally possible and I just need to change the way I think and what kind of strategies I'm using that are going to get me there. I'm just going to work smarter, not necessarily harder and build the infrastructure and systems to achieve that.

I encourage you to dream big. Put big things down on your vision board and goals and put the intention out there – who cares if you aim for the stars and just reach the moon, it still means you have gone pretty far. You must have an aim and an end in mind to strive for.

2. Sacrifices have to be made at times. Focus to grow to new levels and understand that each level of growth in your business financially, requires a different level of thinking. To get to a $100,000 coaching business required me to fill my coaching practice with one-on-one clients and I was there. But to get to a million-dollar business I could not do just one-on-one. The level of thinking I needed was to move away from one-on-one and completely transition out. Just like you transition out of a day job into a business, this was now the stage to transition out of the business one-on-one and to a business that does one-to-many. If I want to do a million dollars a month, I would need to transition from a lot of offline stuff to fully online still one-to-many and get a larger sales team rather than me being the solo person who does the sales and marketing and the face-to-face stuff.

Different levels of thinking are required at every stage of growing a business if you want it to be bigger financially. Along the way I've had mentors and those mentors have taught me how to think differently according to the goals I wanted to achieve. The most important thing about a mentor is to make sure you hire someone who has got the results that you're looking for. This way they can guide you to break through those next levels. Another important thing is to surround yourself with people who are getting those next level results and learn from them, because they're already at that type of thinking and strategic level of having a business at a level that you want to achieve. Yes, there are sacrifices along the way. Is it worth it? Absolutely. Is it hard? Yes, of course it's hard, but it is the journey that is most important to be enjoyed. Because when you get there, like I did, to that $100,000 a month level you celebrate for a few moments and then you go, 'Wow, that really happened to me?' Now what's next? Our growth financially is a reflection of how many people we have actually helped. The more you grow financially, the more people you add value to their life.

If we think about Bill Gates or Steve Jobs, they grew amazing computer companies in Microsoft and Apple and through that so many computers were developed for us to use at home and to be able to grow our businesses. That's what adding value is about. They deserve to be billionaires, because they were clever enough and worked hard to think of a way to make other people's lives easier. Most businesses are started to help people have an easier life in some shape or form.

For us, Ultimate 48-Hour Author is a solution for others to not go through the hard, arduous and time-consuming way people used to write books. We developed a revolutionary blueprint that helps people execute their books in just 48 hours as well as get them out there as soon as possible to build leverage and to have a better life, because they become more successful and credible in their own business.

The financial results are a reflection of how many people we have helped. There is a famous saying that goes, 'The more people you help achieve their dreams in life, your dreams will be taken care of'. This is exactly what financial statements or records are for, to help show you where you're at with your business.

3. If you want to get to a large business, whatever that is in your mind, you need to learn to let go. Outsource and delegate as you go along. Originally it started out with just me and it was just me until I got to the six-figure mark. Then my husband quit his day job because he needed to come on board and help me. Then we started to require experts to help us with our Facebook advertising so we hired a person who does all our Facebook advertising. Two years ago I hired my first virtual assistant, whom I waited way too long to hire. She is a full-timer on our team who takes care of all the online admin remotely from the Philippines. Then there are other contractors who come in and help us for different areas of expertise that we need. In due course we are going to build a sales team.

All of these things have evolved and grown and this way we are able to provide better customer service, and better responsiveness to our customers. We have also outsourced our household duties. We have a cleaner who comes in and different contractors who have helped us get our house as we want it. We have paid a little bit extra to save time because that's our most precious commodity. When you run a business you tend to have a lot less time than people who just go to a 9-5 job and they can do their household tasks outside of that.

Don't wait too long to start outsourcing, take the leap, you will fill the gap. Often it's scary, because you think, 'Oh my god if I need to pay someone full time each week, how am I going to do that?' But when you create the gap, you will figure out how to fill that gap and you will also earn back more time, which will allow you to spend more time in sales looking for new business and new contracts therefore taking your business to the next level.

Just say yes and then work out how. Worst-case scenario you might need to let go of that person if you don't think it's possible and you can't afford to keep them.

Francesca Moi, who wrote *Bums on Seats* with me, is the best outsourcer I've ever met. She outsourced pretty much within a couple of months of starting her business. Even though she wasn't financially ready to. By doing that she now has a team of 7–10 people who are working for her. She also finds it a lot more enjoyable, because the team is working on the same goals and it's a whole lot of fun doing it together.

A lot of people come up to me and say, 'But Nat, I'm not driven by money', well I respond with, 'Money is just a reflection of how many people you have helped'. You may just be framing money in a negative way and giving it a negative meaning, but I believe it's a full representation of how many people you've helped and how much value you're bringing into this world.

If you're one of these people who doesn't want to sacrifice a bit of time away from your family, because that's super important to you, I generally say, 'Look, this is only a sacrifice for a short period of time and what is having your dream life worth when you can have it as you want it for the rest of your life?' Once you create the systems and infrastructure for your dream business and invest some time and effort at the front end it really is a short period of time in hindsight to the lifetime of enjoyment and resources it will provide you in return.

Let's address those of you who are control freaks. I'm also sometimes a control freak and don't trust that others will do as good a job as I can. I had to stop and think about – what is my health worth? Because if I burn out, then this is going to stifle my business' growth and I won't have the strength required to build a super successful business. You will need to engage other people who have strengths you don't so you can grow to the next level. Also other people in your business can be utilised for masterminding and coming up with new innovative ideas. Innovation is the bloodline of having a successful business that thrives.

Let's link this to building your business empire:

1. Growth happens over time. You'll learn, you'll evolve and you'll change the way you think. Each level of growth requires a new level of thinking.
2. Start outsourcing as soon as you have tasks that bog you down and steal your time.
3. Think long-term gain. Your family will be grateful for the lifestyle you can provide in due course.

> "Successful people make money. It's not that people who make money become successful, but that successful people attract money. They bring success to what they do."
> Wayne Dyer

HIS

One thing I always saw growing up was that money came easier for some people than others. My mother's two brothers and their families both had what seemed at the time lots of money. Homes in Melbourne's affluent suburbs, private school for the kids and even holiday homes. We didn't have those things and struggled day to day with my mum working long hours to support us.

Natasa and I both come from a working class background, both children of divorced parents and both being shown that you have to work hard, and work lots to get money to survive. We both had retail management positions when we met and between our salaries and bonuses, we were earning a reasonable income and could do what we wanted to most of the time. We went out to dinners, clubs and went away for weekends and travelled frequently. Thinking back we would've had a combined $140,000 income that for most childless couples was above average.

We never really spoke about money (I've learnt this is very common) or what we would do in the future if we had kids or wanted to retire. Most people put their head in the sand and think ignorance is bliss. We weren't even looking for a business opportunity at that stage until Specsavers came knocking at my door offering a chance to 'buy in' to one of their first stores as an owner. I was guaranteed the same salary I was earning at OPSM with shareholders profits to be paid out after the initial loans were paid off. It cost me $40,000 to buy into the Specsavers a good of amount of which was covered with my cashed out long service and holiday leave I had accrued with OPSM.

It is interesting how you make do with what you have. We had been able to buy our first house together and pay a mortgage and still travel. Sure, houses weren't the price that they are today but it was still a big investment. Even with the new business we decided to buy our second property with pretty much the same income we had. That was more of a stretch but we still made it work. We were cruising through life paying into our superannuation and paying off our primary residence. When I lost the business that was when things became scary for me, as we had started doing our numbers and knew what income we needed to stay above water.

Although I was able to find a job quickly and replace my salary, that month of uncertainty was the catalyst that drove Natasa to start her entrepreneurial journey. She never wanted to rely on anything other than herself to be financially secure. Some would say starting a business is more of a risk than a 'safe' job but seeing people lose their jobs from so called 'safe' jobs all over the world with economic downturns, being your own boss ended up the best option.

Natasa initially wanted to be able to secure a good income on part time hours so she could work around the kids and my work schedule and never could imagine the business like it is today. It was the marketing of 'earn six figures working part-time from home' that first had her choose to complete a life coaching degree and take those first steps towards the global business that our 'Ultimate World' empire has become.

The saying 'money makes money' is so true. When you don't have it, investing back into your business is very tough and when you do finally crack the code and start bringing in good money, it is so much easier to make even more. Although I hear many people say, 'It isn't about the money', it actually is because without money, it is very difficult to 'help' those people who you want to help.

Money is just an object used to exchange value between two parties and the more value we were able to provide, the more money we were able to make and then we could really start to do some good things in the world. When we were on track for our first seven-figure year in the business in year four, we sat down and enjoyed a nice glass of red and were thankful that my biggest stuff up had proved to be our biggest blessing as it showed us the way to another life that we would never have known.

We are consistently working smarter and have continued to grow and achieve seven figures the subsequent two years and we are spreading ripples of good around the world with the people our authors touch with their message. We are told we are lucky, that there are two of us but we get out what we put in and we are fortunate that we can work together with complimentary skills that make each other valuable to our business.

We haven't set a limit to what we can or want to achieve financially because just a few short years ago $100,000 was a goal that we were unsure the business could achieve. We have a team around us that takes some of the workload off us with our VA taking care of a lot of our admin work, and an Ads manager filling our events with our ideal clients.

What we do know is that whatever we do we will do on our terms and we have some non-negotiables, which is our family time and vacation time. I must admit at times my mind wanders and I find myself thinking is $5M enough? $20M? Does it just become a number at that point? People overestimate what they can achieve in a short period of time (such as a month) but underestimate what they can achieve in a longer period of time (such as five years). All I do know is that it will be one hell of a fun ride.

> **Secret Men's Only Section**
>
> Here are some things to think about with your relationship with money:
>
> 1. How would you feel if your girlfriend or partner made more money than you did? Would it make you feel like less of a man or would you celebrate their success?
>
> 2. How many people do you owe money to or how many people owe money to you? Even if it is $5 or $20 this can determine your relationship with money – my advice, immediately call in or pay all of those debts and make that something that you no longer do.
>
> 3. Spend some time thinking about the future and what you will need to live into retirement without relying on pensions or government support because I can tell you one thing, that support either won't happen or it will be so minute that it won't help.
>
> 4. Once you do step three above, initiate a conversation with your partner about your future and what are some of the things you can do together to plan for the future. If you don't think they are already thinking about it, you have obviously forgotten how a woman's brain works!
>
> 5. Get a money clip and load it up with fresh, crisp $50 bills – have as much in there as you want to earn in a single day. Start to feel what it is like to be in possession of money and watch what happens to your life.

Chapter 8
Connecting Through Travel Adventures

HERS

> "Each day of our lives we make deposits in the memory banks of our children."
> Charles R. Swindoll

Entrepreneurs work four times as intensely than employed people, therefore they should allow up to four times the amount of time off recharging and resetting, so that they can keep going at the same pace. Think about your life when you were an employee versus the time and effort that you invest within your business now. For many there ends up being no switch-off button and their business becomes all consuming. You need to have an off-switch for you to be able to achieve life balance, but also to continue having that zest and passion for your business.

When you take time off for holidays, you will also end up having a lot of fun, reconnect at a deeper level with your partner and your children. You'll also build those lifelong memories, which are just so much more valuable than the financial gains that you get just continuously going on and on with your business.

You will in turn get recharged and refired about your business. Often when we come back from holidays, we end up implementing and starting new ideas that have come to us, because taking time off for holidays boosts our creativity and gives birth to new ideas.

I say the spontaneity gives birth to creativity. In our week-to-week schedules, we tend to have a lot of focus time. In my world, I work Monday through to Thursday; I do very long days. That's what I call focus time where you're there, actively working on the tasks that need to be done to keep the business moving forward. Yet on Fridays, Saturdays, Sundays I have nothing scheduled in my planner.

Those are the times where spontaneity can occur. Whether I feel like working on my business or just purely chilling out with my family in whatever I choose to do in those times. If we don't take the time to have a break and switch off from our entrepreneurial lifestyle, burnout can very quickly become a reality and that zest we used to have when we started can start to dissipate. We might also start feeling like we aren't as passionate as we used to be about the things that we're doing in our business.

Ultimately this leads to disconnection from ourselves, the business, our partner, our children and makes us miss out on those finer things in life. If you don't take the time off, you will not have a sustainable way of continuing to build and evolve your business and yourself as a person because you will simply burn out.

When you take time off to stop and recharge and reconnect with your loved ones, especially taking time for self care, it's really important that you realise that this is a way of you rewarding yourself for all the hard work that you're doing. So, how do you achieve this?

If you keep saying, 'I should have taken a holiday', 'I haven't done that for a long time' yet you never schedule it in; it's unlikely it's ever going to happen. My first tip for you in this chapter is to ensure that when you are planning your full year, I recommend planning your year in August-September the previous year, that you schedule holidays first on that annual planner.

You have to think about school holidays if you have children, if you don't like to take your kids out of school too much, depending on their age. With our family we don't mind taking them out of school for a few weeks out of the year, because our kids are very little and in primary school. Everyone's situation is different. Make sure you take that into account and mark that off school holidays in your calendar.

Then discuss with your family where you guys want to go and what you want to see that following year. Plan that out ahead of time as well. This will give you so many things you can look forward to as you work towards those trips and times away to reconnect.

Sometimes throughout the year you'll need to think about whether you guys are going to do some regular trips. In our family, when New Year's Day hits, we go away on a two-week road trip anywhere within 10-12 hours of driving from our home city of Melbourne. We either go towards South Australia or New South Wales and we go in our car because we like to stay one week in one place, by the sea, and another week in another place and then we come home and that's when our year officially begins. The kids are only about 7–10 days from starting the school year, so the timing works well.

Is there a regular trip that becomes kind of a tradition that you take each and every year? You remember what you do and you go and explore different places, but it's of that same flavour. For us, it's that road trip. Every year we always go somewhere on a big trip overseas; exploring a different country and taking a month off, during the year. That's also a regular thing and every time we sit down to plan, we always ask each other what is it that we want to do.

Next discuss with your family where you want to go. There's so much information on the Internet that you can explore. You can cross-check flights. Of course if you know exactly where you're going and what you're doing, you can find the best prices well ahead of time. If you book early you're going to get the best deal on flights as well as accommodation.

Stuart and I share the responsibility of booking trips, so I'm more in charge of the booking of the flights and finding good deals with flights and Stuart's in charge of finding awesome accommodation and great deals for our family of five.

Being a family of five can be quite challenging, you always have to find town houses, apartments or houses that have 2–3 bedrooms to accommodate the family comfortably. That might take a little bit of time, but once you know what you're looking for, you'll be able to understand what to find. I have to say that Stuart does an amazing job. Every time we walk into a place he has found something that really suits the size of our family.

Think about houses, villas, and things like that. I would probably steer away from hotel rooms, because you'd need two separate hotel rooms, which can escalate the price.

When you go on trips, hiring a car is going to move the family around a lot easier and you'll have a lot more choice when you choose to just pick up and go. We always choose to do this so we aren't relying on taxis (unless in South East Asia) and we can really explore different areas.

The other thing when it comes to holidays, depending on who you go with, is to make sure you build a family routine while you're traveling for your holiday. Whenever we're traveling on long haul flights, or a long time in the car, when we get to our destination, the kids can be very tired. The adults can be a little bit more frustrated or on edge if things don't get sorted out quickly, so we sit down and have a rest. We had noticed that we always got into fights the minute we got to our destination. So we have a rule while traveling that we try to catch ourselves the moment we start getting grumpy so that it doesn't turn into a fight.

Now we have a no fights rule, because we understand that we're tired and we're a bit shorter tempered. Therefore we go, okay, it's because we're tired, and we're feeling like this, when we have a good sleep the following day, everything will be back to normal. It works and we always remind each other if someone starts to snap at someone else when arriving at our destination. We remind ourselves that this is to do with the travel, not with being annoyed with the other person.

Then here are some other routines to think about whilst on holidays:

We still have a baby and we've had a baby who sleeps in the middle of the day most of our holidays for the last ten years. We have the routine of going out for an outing in the morning, coming back for a 2–3 hour rest when everyone just does whatever they want, when the baby's asleep. Then we go out in the afternoon and take turns. We sometimes travel with my mum and that way Stuart and I can go on dates in the evening when the kids go to sleep or my mum and I can go out. We just keep switching around and sharing the load.

When travelling with other people, the couples can help you have more time with your partner for some dates. It can be a lot more fun when you're in a group situation. Another thing that we do really quickly is figure out whether we're going to cook for ourselves on a particular trip. I'm now in the US writing this book, and we don't want to be eating out every single meal, so we find the best local supermarket. Immediately we go and shop up some of the stuff that we like to eat and we cook and create a routine, just as we would have at home. Kids are always hungry and going out every five minutes buying stuff is not really the best option. Your money can be used in other areas, for example exploring and having adventures outside of just eating out all the time.

We unpack our things and then shop. We like to unpack everything so it has a spot. It's like we move in properly without living out of a suitcase. Even if it's a one or two night stay, we move in properly. We set ourselves up and then it feels like we're at home and we know where everything sits and we have a routine.

I also check in with the business. I check in with my social media and my emails, once or twice a day, or every two days depending on what we are doing. I still feel like I am away, I am switched off but only check in if I choose to. What that keeps doing though, is let people know at home what's happening, as well as the people watching the journey in my business. People really follow the type of lifestyle that we live and are inspired by it. They like to follow our journeys and our stories that we share throughout our holidays.

Then when we get home there are lots of points of conversation with them. Some people will say, 'That's all well and good Nat, but I'm scared of traveling with my kids, they're so young. It's really hard to travel with kids', and yes absolutely, it is hard. It's not for the faint hearted. But when you have a plan, you have your checklists, when you have everything down pat and you just understand that it's the transit time that's hard, the actual time when you are on holidays is pretty easy and totally worth it. Once you set up your routine and move in as if it's your home, then everything rolls out pretty smoothly so it's really only the transit time that's the hardest.

Also ask yourself, how much do you want to travel? Are you one of those people, like us that does like to be in different locations to expose the children to different cultures? We believe they learn and they explore so much more than just being in the school systems that are so antiquated in Australia. We think giving them that global perspective and experience in different cultures is also going to make them more independent and able to adjust to different situations in the future.

We look at travel not just for pleasure, we look at it as an education and we understand that it's the transit time that's the hardest. We really enjoy and remember all of the memories that we have built together. If you are not at a stage of your business where you can afford to travel as far and wide as we do, as it can be expensive to take the whole family away, take smaller trips.

Earlier on in the business, you can still do things in your local area, even if it's camping. That's all we used to do in the first two years of my business. We used to go away camping a lot on long weekends and that was really inexpensive. It was just to change the scenery, to give us a place to be out of our normal day-to-day surroundings and shake things up and get a little bit more creative and spontaneous.

There is always a way and once you can afford it, then of course go overseas. For those of you who may be scared to lose the momentum from your business when you are away, I say it's only a fear. Often your business will actually skyrocket when you get home, because you're so much fresher and you'll have this new surge on your return, especially if you build up the momentum right before you go.

Often what I do is I try to build up tons of momentum just before I go overseas and then it carries me through till the time that I come back.

Let's link this up to building your business empire:

1. Holidays freshen you and your business outlook and motivation.
2. Holidays create quality time with your family you will remember forever.
3. Holidays are spontaneous time, which will boost your creativity and evolve your business to the next level.

> "Fill your life with experiences not things. Have stories to tell not stuff to show."
> Unknown

HIS

Travel creates memories unlike anything else and us Denman's have certainly proved that to be the case. From the day Judd was born, we have never let the business or the fact that we have had young kids be an excuse to not travel.

I never got on a plane until I was 25 years of age. The only trip overseas was to New Zealand to visit a work colleague and family there for a week. When I met Natasa, being European and hearing her travel stories almost made me a touch nervous. She had travelled back to Macedonia and Europe regularly and very soon we started talking about holidaying together once things became serious.

When Natasa decided that it was going to be Europe, I said my prayers and decided that it may as well be now or never. Growing up in Melbourne's Eastern Suburbs seemed far removed from travelling through Macedonia, Turkey, Greece and France but, like happens to most, that was the trip that well and truly ignited my travel spark. Travelling as a couple was easy. We both liked to do similar things so we never argued about destinations or activities when we were abroad.

When we started our family, the first thing that we agreed on was that having kids wouldn't change the way we travelled and we would get them used to travelling at a young age. So many people told us that it was 'unfair' on the kids to make them travel when they are so young but we ignored them, as it was only parents that hadn't travelled with their children that were so against the idea.

Kids get a basinet on most planes, sleep almost every flight and you get help in almost every country in the world. Kids can almost make travelling easier with express check-ins, offers of assistance, etc. When I have travelled with our kids alone, I am treated like royalty. They still think it is rare for a man to travel alone with kids so I take every advantage that is given to me and lap it up.

When we travel, we make sure that the kids get to experience other cultures as much as possible and we are constantly teaching them about new things. The school they miss is nothing compared to the education they receive when overseas and even their teachers have always blessed their travel adventures and not wanted them to do anything other than complete a travel journal to share with the class on their return.

We travel overseas every year, our favourite places being Thailand, Greece and Italy and do several interstate trips as well as many weekends away. We would much rather spend money on travel and experiences than what Robert Kiyosaki calls 'do-dads' as we know those family memories will last forever.

We have been fortunate that things have never gone pear-shaped and we have avoided trouble, illness and all other such misadventures. However, if they did, travel insurance is a must. Be smart about what you do and the risks you take. Be good to the locals, in fact be good to everyone when you travel as a smile and gratitude goes a long way in any language. The world is becoming more dangerous if you read everything you see on the news. Terror warnings and increased crime, to name a couple, have stopped a lot of people making the decision to travel abroad and I won't tell you otherwise.

All I will say is make sure you do take whatever holidays you can afford to take. If you are a business owner or entrepreneur, it is critical to the success of your business let alone your sanity. You will reconnect with your partner and your children and recharge your batteries so you can operate at your peak performance. If you think you can't afford to take holidays, I know you can't afford not to!

Weekends away are a great place to start. You can camp in the warmer months, not our style but kids love it. Or you can do what we do and hire a house through Stayz or Airbnb. We always manage to find a house for between $150–$200 a night anywhere in Australia (and we need a three-bedroom with our three kids, so it is cheaper if you only have one or two kids) if you bother to spend about an hour looking. We like to choose different locations each time so we have a new area to explore and love to be by the beach, even in the colder months, so The Mornington Peninsula and Surf Coast in Victoria get a great workout.

We might choose to eat out only one night and all these places are self-catered if you need to look after the money expenditure. There are plenty of free activities if you use your imagination and the kid's just love being with you so if you struggle to find the time at home with your busy life, simply kicking the footy or playing a board game will delight them. Take them for a walk on the beach and look for the prettiest shell or the shiniest stone – all of this costs nothing.

Secret Men's Only Section

Here is my guide to making the most out of your holidays:

1. Beer is really cheap in almost every country other than Australia and can be bought almost anywhere. It is also acceptable to crack a can before midday whilst on holidays if the temperature is over 30 degrees Celsius.

2. Your partner is more relaxed and in their creative space when they are on vacation and in this state they are more open to 'after dark activities', sometimes even before dark …

3. If your wife is the cook at home, and she is no good, you get to eat food cooked by others who do it for a living the entire holiday.

4. If you are the cook at home, you get out of cooking for the entire holiday.

5. Holidays give you the chance to wear nothing but board-shorts, singlets and flip-flops for weeks on end. And that my friend is worth it right there!

Chapter 9
Getting Shit Done Fast

HERS

"The way to get started is to quit talking and begin doing."
        Walt Disney

You probably feel like life can't get any busier right now and being a parent of young children (and most likely in the middle-aged bracket) you may also have aging parents that you might need to look after. You are living in the busiest time of your life. Becoming more effective and saving time and being successful to create the safety net that you need for retirement is something that's most likely on your mind.

I created this chapter so that you can gather some tools to get more done in less time. You can have it all, because it is possible once you systemise your life and your business so that it can run like a well-oiled machine. Also these skills will then be transferable to your children, as well as your business and personal life – you will end up thriving.

One of the biggest mistakes we make, especially women, is to pride ourselves on being amazing multitaskers. However, multitasking is completely misunderstood in terms of its effectiveness. Yes, we do need to do it from time to time, but absolutely not all of the time. If we can minimise it to 80% being focused and completing one task before starting the other and then 20% multitasking then we'd have much better results in life.

There is an exercise that you might want to try yourself. It goes something like this: Write out the sentence, 'Multitasking is a waste of time' and then write, while timing yourself, each letter followed by a number, for example, write M and then 1 and then U and 2 and then 3 and L and so on. 'Multitasking is a waste of time' the full sentence is 26 letters.

Time how long it takes you to do one number, one letter and then start again and the second time around write out a whole sentence, 'Multitasking is a waste of time' and then write out the numbers one through to 26. What you will notice is a significantly big difference between the amount of time that it took you to write it out separately than one after the other. Which is something that also shows in life if we're going from task to task, without actually completing one from start to finish, we become less productive and we don't actually have that commitment to completion.

If we don't look for ways to be more productive, we can end up fluffing around, playing the perfectionism strategy that is looping insanity and we can procrastinate. You won't look as good towards your clients or suppliers if you're not getting things handed in or responding to them as quickly as possible. Others will get in before you because of your lack of responsiveness and you won't end up reaching some of those big goals that you have set for yourself in your life and business.

Time is the most precious commodity that we have. Most of us waste so much time just fluffing around and doing things that are not urgent or unimportant. We all have the same 24 hours a day so we need to use them wisely and that is the biggest challenge that mumpreneurs like myself have. Often I get asked the question, 'Nat, how the hell do you do it?' This is how, what I'm about to reveal to you may seem simple, but it requires focus, consistency and obviously follow through.

My step number one is to plan, plan, plan. As there are so many queries around how I plan my time, my weeks, and my year. In 2016 I designed the very first Ultimate Success Planner. If you're interested in having a look into what this planner is about, go to natasadenman.com and you'll be able to scroll through my website and find it.

I put it together so that people could model and replicate what I was doing and how it worked amazingly for myself and I also provide training as to how to use that particular planner. I use this as my crutch and refer to it every single day and I love having a planner that has a layout that's in vertical alignment and week per view. This allows you to see what you have in the mornings, middle of the day and evenings and the tasks that you need to achieve, and your goals. It will also hold you accountable on exercise as well as attendance at networking events, which is super important for us to grow our businesses.

Plan, plan, plan is number one and thinking well ahead of time. Clustering those activities in the planner that are in a similar genre, if you like, and obviously setting aside when you're going to have your time and holidays.

The second thing I do, which is something that I don't see many people do is to create a buffer, buffer, buffer around my events.

I have always been a person who builds in extra buffers to ensure that I don't end up running late somewhere. I don't like nasty surprises. I try to arrive at events about an hour and a half, almost two hours before my guests are due to arrive, so that I can be in the area, parked and if I'm not allowed to walk in at least I know that I'm there and nothing will go wrong.

Recently I was in San Diego about to run a workshop. I didn't realise it but there was a marathon in the area and we couldn't get the car through to get to the venue, so we were about one kilometre away. As we had an hour and a half to figure out how to get to the venue and to let the participants know so they don't get stuck on the road like us, we had enough time to get it all sorted out and start that event on time with everyone there without any issue.

This is why you should allow that extra time for surprises that could really have a detrimental effect on your event. Not so much those business things, but the things where we need to be at different places as a family, or we need to attend appointments with the children. I have never been late for an appointment because of my children.

A lot of parents tend to use that as an excuse (the kids). I just start getting ready super early. It doesn't matter if we arrive early and we're at places just sitting or walking in earlier or wait for our turn. I now see that my children also don't like being late and they start to almost stress out a little bit if they are cutting it fine. It's something that I had instilled in me by my father; he was like a Swiss clock always arriving at places right on or before time. That was something he highly valued and I definitely want to impart that onto my children, because it's a great trait to have and that shows reliability, commitment and respect towards other people.

The third thing that I do is project, project, and project. Project into the future. I design my future. I plan my following year before it has started usually in June-July of the previous year. This is especially important if you have events or conventions that you want to attend. You want to design your business so that there's no ad hoc marketing and that everything that you set and lay out is actually pre-planned and you know what's coming and you have that end in mind of how everything is going to unfold.

Our USA trip was planned well ahead, eight months ahead of time, and that's how long it took to get everything pulled together and to execute a successful first time, international travel for our brand *Ultimate 48-Hour Author*.

Things can change and that is fine, you can always handle changes. Have your planner 80% organised and allow 20% for flexibility. Businesses need a plan, a family needs a plan. If you try to do ad hoc marketing and ad hoc holidays (which never happen) it's like playing Russian Roulette – you never know what will happen next. That is why I say, always, always the first thing you do is put your holidays in your planner.

Some of you may like to think of yourself as a spontaneous person. You like to go with the flow; all of this sounds very rigid. I'll say, look, some of your time will need to be planned and focused. After all, business is about having systems and having consistency towards your clients, so in my world Monday to Thursday is quite planned out and then Friday to Sunday is fun and spontaneous and that's where the creativity comes in.

When you have your business to run throughout the year, you're focused and you go away on holidays and travel with your family.

Then you have your creative time and you're more in flow and you have the spontaneity to do whatever you want.

Often people complain that others make them late: 'It's not my fault, it's the children or my partner, she or he always runs late'. So remember that buffers are super important and can account for those people or situations that make us late. Tell them you need to be somewhere half an hour to 45 minutes before you really have to and then you'll end up arriving on time.

If you feel like planning your business really far in advance is too far away, then maybe consider why that is so important. Having a steady and consistent business and revenue is one of the most important things that you can do for your family, but also for your emotional wellbeing. It can be very stressful if your leads dry up, if you're not getting enquiries. That will only happen if you don't have a projected plan. You need to know what you're doing and where you're going and who you're going to meet with and where you're going to generate the opportunities that are going to result in your business being financially viable.

Plans can change, but you need to start at least with something to set some intention and please by all means stay focused.

I want to finish off this chapter with this statement: *'There isn't a lack of ideas, but there is a lack of focus'*. I'm currently in the US, while writing this book. I can see how many choices there are and how many people are everywhere. Being in a busy city right now like New York City is increasing my stress levels. I always say, 'A confused mind will always say no'. For example, I've walked into a food place and I'll go, 'Oh my god, I don't know what to choose'. There's just way too much to choose from and I don't want to do it.

That's the same thing in business and life. If we overcomplicate our lives and don't keep things simple then we don't actually stick at things and get good at one thing and create a successful business.

Make your life simple. That is actually the secret to being happy, to being able to make good choices, to being able to make good money and support your family, as well as for your family to be clear on what it all involves and how we operate as a unit together.

Focus is important whether you're talking about management or family, or management of the business or with your life. Remember we are all creative creatures, as human beings, so there's no lack of creativity, there's a lack of focus. When you focus and keep it simple, that's where you will see your life skyrocket and you will be happy about the thing that you stand for and what you offer to others.

Let's link this to building your business empire:

1. Steady business works with plans, goals, buffers and projections.
2. Spontaneity can exist even if you plan.
3. Your children will model your time management traits, so make sure you model the positive and resourceful time management traits.

> "Productivity is never an accident. It is always the result of a commitment to excellence, intelligent planning and focused effort."
> Paul J. Meyer

I always thought that I had a good ability to get things done in a timely manner. Until I met Natasa. I never missed a deadline all through my school days and in my working and management roles. Sure, I may have had to pull a few all-nighters or have the performance appraisals in on the actual day they were due, but I was proud that I was able to get things done when they were due.

It didn't take me long to see the difference between how I managed my time and how Natasa managed her time. It started back when Natasa and I were managing competing OPSM stores. We would always have reports that needed to be sent to our state boss, Bernadette, and we could see when each store had these completed. There was never a week when OPSM Epping wasn't the first. Now, Epping wasn't quieter than the other stores, in fact pro-rata they were one of the busiest, but that store was just better organized than all the others.

At the monthly meetings, most other managers were making excuses about why they hadn't got their reporting done, or had not met their set budgets. Natasa and I had not only smashed our budgets but also managed to get our reporting in before others had (or had not even bothered).

Before kids, we managed our time really well and never used 'lack of time' as an excuse to not do something. After kids, we managed our time even better and as babies love routine, we saw the benefits in their early years and how settled they were. After kids and with a business, now that is when you need to manage your time to 'Get Sh1t Done'.

One of the foundations that we have set for the business is that we deliver what was promised on time, if not early every time. If someone wants a quote, it will be done within 12 hours. If we say we will ring at 2.45pm, we will be ready to dial at 2.44pm. Every email or enquiry will be responded to within 24 hours, rain, hail or shine.

This type of service doesn't happen much these days and we have found that people appreciate it. In 2015 we bought our dream house and wanted to landscape it and build an oasis for our family and ourselves. This meant dealing with a number of tradesmen, contractors and project managers. Not once did we receive anything on time. Not the call-back from the first enquiry, to receiving a quote, even us wanting to get invoiced so we could pay them seemed like pulling teeth. Every agreed deadline was missed; every excuse under the sun was given from blaming the 'girls in the office' to 'last night was poker night'.

Australian's see being 'busy' as a badge of honour. Listen to anyone asking another how they have been and the most common responses are 'I am flat out like a lizard drinking mate', which translates to, 'I am very busy'.

Interestingly enough, the more I looked into this, the more sinister this response actually is. You see, the busier we say we are, the less we are expected to take on anything else and god forbid do something, anything, else other than what we are doing. There are a lot of successful people who have a time abundance and a lot of unsuccessful people who are 'flat out' all the time but this is due to procrastination, lack of planning and delegation and simple laziness.

I have often been asked how I manage to have the time abundance I do with all the balls I have in the air. It definitely takes some practise but most of all it takes a change in how you think about things. I used to believe that time was unlimited (and money was limited but that is another story for another day) and so I didn't value my time as much as I do now. This couldn't be further from the truth. An example of this is I used to get asked to 'go out for a coffee' from other business people. I was looking at getting more connections and meet more people so I would agree, sometimes driving an hour to meet someone who would either not show up on time or want nothing more than push their agenda onto me, MLM for instance. By the time I ended the meeting and drove home, I could be away for more than four hours – Aaaarrrggggg what a waste of time!

You see, I didn't value my time so why would anyone else? You need to set boundaries around how others can have some of your time. 'Time Vampires' as I like to call them, don't get to have any of my time. My family does, my friends do and my clients do. Negative people don't get any of my time either as I choose to surround myself with like-minded people.

If you are like me and wear many hats: father, husband, son, friend and business owner, you need to get very structured with your day and week. I have found grouping 'like' activities in blocks as switching between 'roles' if you like (so from dad role to business role requires different parts of the brain) so 'switching' or multitasking eats into your day and you will never achieve everything you need to or worse still, you will do both roles poorly.

Also identify when you are most productive. For myself, and thankfully for Natasa too, it is after the kids go to bed at 8pm and we have three solid uninterrupted hours Monday through Thursday to 'Get Sh1t Done'.

> **Secret Men's Only Section**
>
> Here are five ways you can get more 'Sh1t Done' as a man:
>
> 1. Growing a beard saves 3650 minutes a year on shaving – that will enable you to watch 20 extra games of football with the time you save.
>
> 2. Stop trying to prove you are right all of the time. This is time you can spend more productively elsewhere, and it is a fight you can never win so just be happy enough knowing you are right.
>
> 3. Stop multitasking – if you can't talk and breathe, stop doing the least important one. I'll let you decide which one that is …
>
> 4. Learn the 'double bind' technique and use it on your children. Would you like to go to 'the park' or go to 'the play centre' rather than asking them what they want to do!
>
> 5. Perfect the grilled cheese toastie – it can be used as a breakfast, lunch or dinner alternative and takes only minutes to make!

Chapter 10
Leaving Them Home Guilt-Free

HERS

> "Where we love is home – home that our feet may leave, but not our hearts."
> Oliver Wendell Holmes

Expanding beyond your local area can be scary, yet exhilarating at the same time. The hardest thing I have found is saying goodbye to my children each time I go. But then I also think about my big reason why and the purpose that I was put on this earth for. This is the thing that really drives me and keeps my light burning strong, as it expands me and my comfort zone each time I travel.

I choose to travel interstate and globally. Right now I am writing this book from the US. What does travel do for your business? Well it truly grows the brand perception around what you're doing and how big your business is perceived. It teaches you how to learn and stretch out of your comfort zone more and more so that you become a more evolved and confident human being and business owner.

Travelling allows you to really focus and get so much done in your business, because you have got just you on your trip and you can have some really focused and productive time, just some adult time for you.

In terms of family, travelling is so wonderful because coming home is so rewarding. You know the saying, 'Distance makes the heart grow fonder', it's not just a myth. It's actually the truth and you really appreciate seeing your partner, your husband and your children and their smiling faces and seeing how much they missed you and you missed them and getting those extra kisses and hugs when you reunite again.

As your radius expands and as you grow, you will reach further and you will be able to help people on a global scale.

The negative side to traveling is leaving your children home. That's when guilt levels can climb really sky high. It can be super tiring, jet lag can be a bitch and the packing and unpacking can become very tiresome.

Of course dealing with different cultures can be challenging in itself and can really stretch you in terms of doubting what you're doing. A couple of situations I came across in the US, I just felt like at times I could not understand these people, but once I got used to it of course it was just being in a new place and trying to learn about a different culture.

Leaving them at home is not easy but it can be very rewarding for you, your business, and ultimately your family. This is where you truly get to satisfy your desires and make that global impact.

How does a mother of three like myself handle leaving home? We are at the airport often and I do like my family dropping me off and picking me up, because of course my husband is part of the business. That's part of our routine when we I go away alone. If my kids are awake they're so ecstatic and can't wait to meet me and pick me up at the airport when I come home if the time is suitable.

But there are some things to remember that you can do to make this a little bit less full of guilt for yourself:

1. Nowadays there is FaceTime and I can connect with my children and Stuart morning and night and we have lots of regular chats, almost as if we're in the same place. We like doing that. It's part of our routine and we celebrate the successes. If I have successes on my business trip the first people to find out are my children and Stuart. Good things can be happening to me when I'm travelling alone but if I have no one to celebrate with, it can feel kind of blasé. I like to buy my kids little gifts when I'm away. Not every single trip, but if I have the time and I can find something they'll like I bring

them little gifts back. They really appreciate it, the little ones. I give it to them in the car as we're driving back home after they pick me up from the airport and it puts a smile on their faces.

2. We talk about the future things that we have to look forward to together. I usually have one-on-one dates with my children, especially if I've been away. I come home and organise a few different things with each of them. We talk about our holidays and what we're going to do and we daydream about what's going to happen next time we go away. Whatever we promise, no matter what, that's the number one thing that I have to follow through. I will never say yes to anything that I don't think I can do just to appease them.

For me it's about integrity. If I can say yes we can do this or no we can't, then I will follow through on exactly what I have promised. That's really important to me. I can't go against my word, I can't do it with my clients, I can't do it with my friends and I can't do it with my children. Always commit to something or don't say anything at all or just say no.

3. When you go on your business trips, yes your business will grow but also there are lots of times on that trip that you will have time to yourself. Enjoy that break and get lots done, because often at home we can be quite distracted. I have a house office and when my kids are at home, I kind of feel guilty being tucked away in the office working. I do my best to get most of my work done while they're in school and care. I love using flight time as focus time to get bookkeeping done; other tasks that don't require the Internet and I get really productive on implementing new systems in the business. Often creating new systems requires us to be quite focused and concentrated in terms of typing, creating workbooks or installing new systems into the business to make it more efficient and productive.

I get all of those things done on flights. I always have a plan that I'm going to use that time in transit, even just sitting at the airport, because sometimes you could be waiting for your plane to board for over an hour. That's an hour you can just put your head down into the laptop and get a whole lot done even in hotel rooms. I recently went to Sydney for a wedding and thought I'd do a workshop for authors while I was there. What I try to do in these situations is stay two extra days; and I'm going to spend these two days just to work on my business.

When I knew this Sydney trip was coming up, for two months I wrote down a list of to do stuff at the back of my planner, things I would never get to do in my day-to-day weeks. When I was in my Sydney hotel for those additional two days, I could execute this whole list and get all these things completed so that it can move the business forward and have more infrastructure around it set up.

It worked like magic and I got through that list very easily because I already knew exactly what I needed to do and I just sat down and ticked one thing off after another and I got so much done. I actually love the travel not only just because it grows my business, but it also gives me time to just be really productive. I do my best to just be away during the week, so Monday through to Friday so I'm always home for the weekend. Usually Monday through to Friday, the kids are in their own activities, school, childcare, and after school care and things like that. Whether I'm at home or interstate, it doesn't really matter, because they are doing their own stuff. Then we are back together on the weekend, so it feels like just this week I'm having a week in Sydney or another week it's a week in Adelaide and Perth. I do all my shorter trips that are between 1-4 days during the week. Of course when it's overseas it might be a longer period of time.

I hate seeing the sad look on my kid's faces when I leave. I always do my best to remember that in time, they will be modelling me. If I feel sad, then they will reflect that back at me and if I'm upbeat and happy and excited they will be exactly the same. Watch how you're feeling and what feelings you're modelling when you're leaving them home. If you're acting like, I'm going to miss you so much, you're almost down to tears, then they will probably do the same, they will be mimicking your emotions and how you feel, because that's who they learnt from. Yet if you're excited and you give them an awesome vibe and that it's going to be great for the family and what you will do when you return, then they're also going to be amazing.

Travelling can be very expensive for business and people are often scared to take their business interstate or internationally, because if they don't get a result it can mean that they might be wasting a lot of money.

Again, I say take-calculated risks that won't destroy your business. Start with smaller and closer trips. Use various resources that are now available, like Airbnb to stay in places, Uber instead of normal taxis. Start flying economy to start off with before you upgrade to business or first class. Do all of the things that are clever ways to save hundreds of thousands of dollars and still make those business trips a possibility.

Once you've grown confident enough to know that you can take your business interstate and globally, you will work it out. First of all, see how you're converting in sales at a local level, because if you have your conversions and understand what your average conversion rate is, then generally you would get similar results in other places as well. Once you take those calculated risks, work out ways to do it inexpensively before you can understand how you've gone in that place then you can return time and time in the future, you will get similar results.

That's exactly how I did it initially. I did go in and not get many results. I would put in so much effort, get people in the room, do my workshops and sometimes I would come home totally empty handed. However, nothing beats the experience, nothing beats you going through those first few times. This first time in the US, I didn't even know if I'd sell one thing. My intention was to facilitate five-half day workshops, then invite people into the Las Vegas Ultimate 48-Hour Author retreat a month later. I just didn't know how it would go. Would I inspire the American people? Could they think my program was valuable and worth their investment?

Even though the same workshop has the proven results and has everything going for me in Australia, here I was walking into a cold market, so for me it was a risk. I just didn't know what to expect yet I did a six-figure trip, because I took that risk. I also spent $30-$40,000 to make it happen and to get my business to the international stage, if you like.

If you miss your family a lot when you're away, take them with you sometimes. Block out the business time and then have the holiday with them. That's exactly what we're doing right now and that's often what we do when we go to Queensland. I did two weeks of business here and I spent a few days by myself on my 40th birthday in New York, which was really lovely and then I met my family back in LA and we were on a month-long holiday.

Then we will finish it off with the retreat in Las Vegas that I mentioned before. Then we go to Queensland (Australia), for ten days with the family, work in the business 2–3 days and then fly back home. It's a great way to take them along for the ride. Part of that trip will be tax deductible through the business and it's just a great way to make more memories and have more time with each other and just enjoy it.

Let's link this up to your business empire:

1. Focus on the future and the opportunities that travel provides.
2. Remember you can take your family along on some of your trips and have an awesome holiday at the same time.
3. Taking time away a few times a year is the most productive way for you to work on your business so that it grows to the next level.

> "There are not perfect parents, and there are no perfect children, but there are plenty of perfect moments along the way."
> Dave Willis

HIS ♂

I actually can't remember the first time I was left at home with Judd, and that is how I know that everything went smoothly. There are so many things that happen along this parenting journey that unless it was downright hard or gorgeously cute there is a parenting fog that covers most of the other 'stuff'.

I know I must have been a touch nervous about the sleep and feeding routine as everything else I already had well under control. I have heard of some dads who don't hear their baby crying at night, which as a light sleeper and a realist, I don't know if I believe them. So in my case, I knew that I would wake to feed Judd without him needing to take it up to maximum decibels.

It really wasn't until after Mika was born that Natasa really started travelling more for business and it still was only randomly. After Xara was born this is when her travel and our separation was more prevalent. I remember Natasa wanting to attend the Professional Speakers Association conference in Canberra when Xara was very little (about three months old) and as we were able to get our older two looked after as it was a weekend, I flew up with her and almost acted as a wet nurse. Well not quite, but feeding her expressed milk in between Natasa quickly running back to the room during break times to breastfeed Xara.

It wasn't easy or a fun weekend for me but we did it as I knew the importance of Natasa being able to attend a conference with our ideal clients so I sucked it up and did it. The point I want to make here is marriage is a partnership and there are times that you need to step up, or even step back when the situation arises. It isn't always beer and skittles but then again, life isn't in general. Saying yes to doing the things that we don't want to do, or are initially uncomfortable or downright scared to do is the best thing we can do for our own personal growth.

No matter what we do in our business, we always schedule our big vacations and family time activities before booking Natasa's business travel. Over the past two years, we have done our best to book two distinct 'tours' as such and try to maximize her time away to fit in all her travel into blocks. The first block is booked in for March and the second September. Now these aren't set in stone but things like school holidays, our own travel etc., have made these months work well. In general the longest I am with the kids alone is two-week blocks unless Natasa headed off to Europe like she did in 2016 – that was five weeks.

The kids are already used to this time apart but as they have school, care and me to entertain them, not to mention FaceTime and Skype, there is never a day without them seeing each other and talking. I am not sure how we would've managed years ago without all of this technology but like they did back then, we would make it work. I love having the time alone with the kids as we get to do some different things to what our normal routine is when Natasa is home. Now I am not talking about a bath every week and takeout dinners, but things like Lego building challenges and adventures in the local parks and reserves happen more frequently.

You do have to maintain discipline and parent the same, as when your partner is there as otherwise your kids will start to try to play you off against your partner. They need to know that homework is still done at the same time, evening dinner and bath routine stay the same and bedtime doesn't change. I have seen many dads throw all discipline out the window when their partner is away but that is just asking for chaos and the kids will start thinking it is 'better' when their mum is away.

As parents we also talk to our kids all the time about why our lives (Natasa's and mine) are different to most of their friends as school who have parents who have jobs and work for someone else. We share what Natasa is doing when she is travelling and they excitedly ask after each workshop or seminar she runs, "Mumma, did anyone sign up?" which means did a new author join our Ultimate 48-Hour Author program?

Like all parents, we are doing our best juggling family time, business time, time away and time at home and I am sure that there are times when we could do things better but that is okay. Life isn't about perfection and neither is parenting. We never know the meaning that our kids are giving to a particular situation and even through our education and communication with our kids, we just never know if something so simple that we take for granted is causing our kids stress or to be upset.

What our kids are learning is that as adults, we do need to put ourselves first so that we can provide the best of things to our kids. They are learning that there can be more to life than the traditional 9-5 job and they are learning the entrepreneurial way. They will never be raised to believe that things come easy and Five Star is all there is. Camping at Bonnie Doon will always be a right of passage but most of all they will see that life doesn't need to be lived ordinary.

Secret Men's Only Section

How to survive your partner leaving you alone to look after the kids:

1. The biggest tip I have here is pre-make things that can be eaten over more than one night. Kids are happy eating pasta bake for nights on end. Add in a different salad or veg each night and they will be happy.

2. Stick to the rules, for your partner's benefit and mainly your sanity. You don't want there to be anarchy and chaos when they are away.

3. No matter how the house happens to get while they are away, make sure that there is a calm, clean place to video chat so that they see you are taking care of the kids and for the love of God, clean the house before she returns.

4. Ask your kids if there is something they want to do that they don't normally get to do. It is great to find out if they have any new interests that can be continued when the family is back in their normal routine.

5. Keep the alcohol to a minimum – you are the sole person responsible for their wellbeing. If something does happen, make sure you are in a state to be able to care for them or get them to a hospital if need be.

Chapter 11
Uncovering New Energy Reserves

HERS

> "Time and health are two precious assets that we don't recognise or appreciate until they have been depleted."
> Lucas James

I do 74 minutes of exercise per week. How, you probably think? Well, I have 2 x 30-minute personal training sessions with my personal trainer and then I follow an app called the *7-minute Workout* and I do two of those a week. It really has made a huge difference in my life. At the time of writing this book, I'm coming up to 18 months of consistently doing four lots of this exercise each and every single week, even when I'm on the road and traveling or on holidays. I have not missed a week of doing this in 18 months and I don't intend to.

Why do I do this? Because as I discovered, over the years as I have achieved more success and have become busier in the business, I require more energy to get shit done. I require having a clearer head and health to be at those peak optimal levels and to be able to speak and deliver at 100 events every year as I have done for the last three years in a row.

It makes travelling so much easier, because travel can really take it out of you and ultimately being an entrepreneur, we are our brand. We need to look good for the brand and what we represent and be a living and breathing proof of health and wellness as well. This also allows us to be a great model for our children when it comes to showing we care for ourselves.

The entrepreneurial lifestyle can be without routine, so we must create one for peak performance. If you don't you can very quickly start feeling quite sluggish, look unhealthy, gain weight, your skin can look quite bad, you'll feel run down a lot easier, you'll get colds and flus a lot easier than others and your immunity can go downhill very fast. If you do get sick more often, your results in your business will suffer because your energy won't quite be there and as a parent, you will run out of energy to be able to devote to your kids for that quality time that you guys should be sharing together.

The busier you get and the more success you achieve, you will require more energy to keep up with people and your children. That's why creating a routine for peak performance is key to keep you going at a rate you have to for your business and your family to thrive.

I want to discuss some of the hacks that I use and how I built in this routine for peak performance. If some of these things resonate with you, you can start doing them for yourself.

The number one thing is the morning routine. I tend to work Monday through Thursday quite full on and I have Fridays, Saturdays and Sundays off. My workdays start off in the morning, waking up and listening to a meditation. This is good for my mind and my positivity and my ability to feel great and to start the day in a positive state of mind. I like listening to Ester Hicks. Look her up on You Tube and listen to her morning and evening meditations. That goes for about 9-15 minutes and then I get up and exercise immediately.

If I have a personal training session booked, I will get dressed and go downstairs generally within those ten minutes and finish that and then have a shower and a healthy breakfast before I get going for the day.

If the personal trainer is not coming, the minute I get up, even still in my pyjamas, I jump up and down with the *7-minute Workout* app and then get myself ready. I always feel that everything I need to do to start the day positively is done and therefore I'm able to be more clear-minded and productive as I get on with my day.

The second thing is personal grooming, especially for women, can become quite time consuming. I want to discuss a few things that

I've done over the years to win back more time in my days. First thing we did when we could afford it, we outsourced the cleaning of our home. We have a cleaner that comes once a fortnight to do a deep clean of our whole house. We do touch ups in between and that works awesome for us. Another thing I did to save a ton of time and look great is laser hair removal in all areas I didn't want hair on my body and that has not only saved me time but also money on all the hair removal products and procedures I used to invest in. Recently I also had keratin put through my hair, because being a public speaker I had to have my hair really perfect. As a presenter we need to look our best selves and because I have wavy, almost curly hair, putting the keratin through which smooths it out, allowed me to save so much time in the mornings and when I need to be looking really great. This treatment cut down my hair grooming time by five times. It used to take me 50 minutes to do my hair, it now only takes ten.

Nails can be done with gel or shellac and something that's going to last you a pretty long time and look great if you are in the public eye. These treatments can be expensive but they are mostly once off payments and are totally worth the time that you're going to save that you can use in other ways to build your business.

The other thing that we can do to ensure peak performance and winning that extra time and feeling healthy is to sort out our stuff, systemise and organise our household for a faster approach and access to what we need. People can waste so much time looking for things when they need them. I've had on a couple of occasions hired a personal organiser to come over. I love learning lots of new tips and tricks from them. I am a fairly organised person and organisers love working with me – I'm always open to learning something new. My approach in life is to have a minimalist feel to my home and office. When I travel I don't carry too much stuff. I only take exactly what I need, because being in the business of writing books, I do need to take a lot of sample books with me, which can weigh quite a lot. I've learnt to pack minimally for what I would need for fun, rest, play, and presenting.

We set goals and times to de-clutter the whole home twice a year. Every six months – once in the winter and once around Christmas.

Usually it's when we have time to take a break. This keeps everything intact. If you have growing children, who grow out of a lot of clothes, or certain toys, that allows you to keep your house at the bare minimum of what you need. Generally they say the 80-20 rule applies, meaning that you only use 20% of everything that you have, 80% is just sitting there as stuff.

De-cluttering every six months puts everything in order, makes you look through your things and make some decisions and then you can donate to people who are in need. If you need to move house or find stuff you end up doing it a lot faster and easier and save a ton of time.

Your children get to learn and see this. Often when 1 start my *7-minute Workout*, my little daughters will run in and start doing all the exercises, sit-ups, push ups, wall sit and it's really cute. I even caught my middle daughter Mika in her room one morning as I got up and walked into her room and she was jumping up and down, doing all the different exercises like star jumps and sit-ups. I said, 'What are you doing?' She is only five years old and she said, 'Well I'm exercising, Mama!' For a little girl who doesn't have a lot of co-ordination, she was still modelling what I was doing and I found it very cute and I was proud of the fact that she's seen me do that and then she was wanting to do it for herself.

I always encourage people to keep finding ways to win back time. Things like preparing bulk meals so you don't have to be cooking every single day. Working out who's going to be the person doing the drop offs and pick-ups at school and how you can cluster activities so that you're saving time. We all have the same 24 hours in the day; it's how we use them that matters. Having a household with children, with each additional child, we get more time poor. It's important that we implement systems, because those systems are going to keep us moving and focusing on the things that matter the most.

I meet a lot of people who, like me, hate exercising. As I said, 74 minutes a week is not a lot, but it can keep you fit, healthy and toned. Just so you don't think I'm the super healthiest and fittest person in the world, I used to say that I really hate to sweat. Then I realised that I needed to because, as we get older, our energy levels deplete and I realised if I don't start exercising, I'm going to stiffen up and then everything is going to become a lot harder.

I committed when I joined with my personal trainer that I would be doing this with her for 2–3 years. This is because I learnt from a mentor of mine that it takes 2–3 years or 1,000 times of repetition to build a new neural pathway. I know that this is definitely longer than 28 days (an amount of time often suggested) because previously I had gone on exercise kicks and kept it up for up to 2–3 months and it still didn't stick as a consistent habit.

Now, being 18 months into this journey and having not missed a week of exercise the four times, I feel like I can't live without it. I think my new neural pathway is definitely on the way to being very firm and instilled and I really encourage you to give that a go as well.

Yes, it's a long period to commit to but it's totally worth it if you want to have a habit for life. Be very careful when life does get very busy because your routine can go out of whack and out the window, then you will find it hard to get back in shape.

Simplify your routine and know at times it's okay not to be perfect. Sometimes I won't do the Monday through Thursday exercise, because I'll have a full on day one day and I'll want those extra ten minutes of sleep in and I will just know that I've got seven days and I'll have to make up for then somewhere. And it's totally achievable, it doesn't need to be hours of walking or running, it can be as simple as my 74 minutes.

Having children, especially young children, keeping things organised can be quite hard when others are messing them up. If this is happening in your household and you don't feel like you have the support, then it's really important that you get everyone involved in what I like to call 'mission de-clutter'. This way they will take ownership and they will observe and learn how to de-clutter for themselves later on in life.

What I find with my children is that when we do the mission de-clutter, they start to play a lot more with their toys and you can almost sense that there's this feeling within them that goes, ahh, everything is organised, everything is in its place. They start playing with more things and you can see that they too can feel when things look good and are in their right places, that it's so much easier to access and use them.

Get onto some of these strategies and make them part of your daily, monthly and annual routine.

Let's link this up to building your business empire:

1. Routines not only make children thrive, but adults and businesses succeed because of routines.
2. Clustering activities will allow you to get more done.
3. Your children will learn how to be peak, healthy performers as you lead by example.

> "Fitness: Its not something you achieve and forget, it's something you attain and maintain. Fitness is a lifestyle."
> Bonnie Pfiester

HIS

Anyone who has kids will tell you that there are times when they are so tired that they simply want to sleep for a week. From the lack of sleep when they are very little babies through to the tears and tantrums of a toddler, this period can last more than ten years if you are like us and have had three kids. Kids have boundless amounts of energy and they only have two settings, on and off. When they are on, it is non-stop and they seem like they can go on forever. Then the crash comes and it can be half an hour of hell that seems to last four weeks. And then they sleep, which is the off button.

Natasa and I both decided that we would work around the children's sleep time, especially the day sleeps but most of the time when they are really young, you are just so damn tired yourself, this time isn't that well used. I always feel, as a parent, you are on the entire time. There is no chance to recharge unless you make it. I failed at this for the first five years of fatherhood and probably still do today. The stamp that is across the front cover of this book is something that I need to follow even more.

Unless you are rested and in a good space yourself, you are not going to be the best parent to your kids you can be. If you are not looking after yourself both physically and emotionally, their supercharged energy levels will drain what stamina you will have left. Being a male, and a sufferer of Man-flu that still to this day only affects 49% of the population, there are times when caring for your kids through your own illness just has to be done. So, the less times that you are afflicted with Man-flu the better. This means eating well and making sure that you are physically active.

As this book is all about honesty and the everyday challenges that we all face, I need to share that my self-care is not at the levels it has been and currently should be. I fluctuate between motivated to stay healthy and all consumed with being a dad, husband and business owner that I have to dig well into the reserves to keep all the balls in the air and when one drops, it is the health ball every time.

I am fortunate that I have naturally high levels of stamina; I think that comes from my extroverted introvert personality where I can recharge my energy levels in my own company which I make sure I get enough of. Natasa is the opposite, a full extrovert who gets her energy from others and the stimulation of large groups and exciting activities. She loves being the centre of attention whereas I shun the attention and find myself desperately needing to have my 'me-time'.

My children fill my energy and love bucket up with their unconditional love and except for a built in mute button occasionally, there isn't one personality trait in any of them I would change as they are uniquely themselves.

People say all the time that you can have everything in your life and as much as I accept what they say, I find myself constantly saying, what would I remove from my life to replace with more exercise and wellbeing activities? I asked for and received a Fitbit for Christmas so I can monitor my activity and that has been a great thing to keep me motivated and on track and taking the time out for a brisk walk and aiming to be constantly in motion every hour has me in a good space.

The interesting part of this is that when my motivation to get more active strikes, I can see that the kids suddenly want to start doing more active things with me so that should be motivation in itself to keep it a priority. As business owners, especially in today's world where so much happens online, we live very sedentary lives and unless it is in your focus, it is very easy to put on weight and lose your energy that we all know is required to operate at our best.

I am always asked where Natasa gets her energy from and there is no simple answer to it except she is inspired by life and wants to get as much out of every day as she can. She has the 'achiever pattern' as one of her drivers so unless she achieves something everyday, she can't go to bed satisfied and feels like it is a day wasted. That is pretty strong motivation in itself and when you combine it with an extroverted personality and someone who gets driven by contribution and adds her number one quality in The Milton Strength Finder personality trait as 'WOO' (wining others over) you can see how it happens.

Added to all this is she hired a personal trainer who works with her 2–3 times a week and she commits to five days exercise a week (so an additional two days outside her trainer) to keep her body in the peak shape it needs to be to cope with her travel schedule and other commitments that she has.

Sometimes it is tough to keep all of the balls in the air, I understand that better than most yet as long as your health and wellbeing is somewhere in your focus, you will have the ability to keep taking that one step after the other in a forward direction, which is the key to a prosperous business and life.

Secret Men's Only Section

Here are my top five tips for keeping all the balls in the air without dropping them:

1. Identify your personality type. Once you do this it will help you understand where you get your energy from. Trust me, it isn't always from meeting Azza, Bazza, Muzza and Krackers at the pub.

2. Any movement is better than no movement. If you want to keep yourself a bit more accountable to the minimum recommended daily steps of 10,000, get a Fitbit so that you are no longer guessing.

3. A solid love making session is said to burn 500 calories – I am not sure if they are talking about the average male or some Italian Stallion but hey, it is just my job to report the facts so get to it.

4. There are lighter carb beer options available these days that actually taste pretty good so instead of drinking your daily allowance in beer calories, give a Pure Blonde a try!

5. Play with your kids outside as much as possible. Not only will they always remember the times they played <insert activity here> with Dad, but it will get them out of the house and you more active all while bonding and having fun.

Chapter 12
Seven Communication Secrets Revealed

HERS

> "Communication to a relationship is like oxygen to life, without it…. It dies."
> Tony Gaskins

The most successful people in the world have spent time to learn powerful communication skills that can be understood by most people. It is as essential to have these skills within the family unit as it is if you're running a business, in your career or other areas of your life.

When you do develop your ability to communicate clearly, your family will end up running like a well-oiled machine. You will have a more consistent approach in parenting as well as business. You'll be able to thrive and really smash out your goals. You will role model for your children amazing skills that show them how to be responsive, rather than reactive, and when problems or challenges arise they will be able to solve them a lot faster.

Did you know that communication declines significantly in most relationships, businesses and families over time? Yet it's the key to success in all areas of life. There's an NLP presupposition that says, 'The meaning of the communication is the response that it gets'. If someone does not understand you, it's actually your responsibility to communicate even clearer, or say it in a different way, so that you get a different response.

As a public speaker I know this to be crucial, because if my audiences don't understand or get what I'm saying, I need to be saying it in a different way so that it's understood by the majority of people listening to me.

When I started out on this entrepreneurial journey seven years ago, I read somewhere that there are four stages that people go through if they fail to communicate well. I'll give you an example of what those are. I call them the 4 R's.

Anger can arise, if we don't communicate effectively or at all sometimes in relationships, so we start off visiting the first stage: *Resistance*. Let's use the towel on the bathroom floor as an example. If Stuart was leaving the towel on the bathroom floor all the time after a shower and if I didn't say anything, I would start to have resistance towards him (this usually shows up as slight annoyance). I'd be a little bit pissed off, but I'd pick it up again and again.

If I continued not to say anything and did it ten ... 20... 30 times, I could move into the next stage: *Resentment*. Resentment is when you're just starting to say things to yourself mostly like, I wish he wouldn't do that; I hate it when he does that, without coming out and saying it to him.

Just think there are probably a number of things that our partners do that don't sit well with us. We're using the towel on the bathroom floor as a simple example, but there are other irks that we have with each other that can build up resistances and resentments over a period of time, especially if we don't bring it up with effective communication.

The other stage that this then moves into as time goes on is: *Rejection*. Rejection is when you start dissing your partner in various areas. Whether you stop sharing affection with them, being intimate with them, you just start to feel distant and you're kind of living separate lives.

Once you move past this stage, you go into the worst of the four R's and that is: *Repression*. Repression is when you push everything down and in a way make peace with it, which is a worse stage to live in. This is where people could live for decades repressing a lot of things that they should have just brought up and dealt with in the early days. One day when you see a couple announce that they're breaking up, everyone else around them says, 'Oh, but I thought they were so happy and together'. But it is those people who have generally been living many years in repression.

The good news is there is a way out of repression and that is obviously through communication – and effective communication that does not point the finger or blame other people, but is said in a way whereby the other person takes it in a positive and resourceful way.

If we use the example of the towel and the bathroom floor (by the way this was a real example from our family! It used to annoy me, because he did leave the towel on the floor after every shower). This is how I approached it: I said to him, 'Darl, I know you probably don't realise that you're doing it, but every day when I go into the bathroom, your towel is on the bathroom floor and that kind of annoys me, so I would appreciate it if you picked it up and hung it up, because every time I go in I pick it up and feel annoyed.' What I say is, 'I know you don't realise that you're doing it,' rather than going to him, 'Can't you just pick up your towel from the floor after a shower? You know it's so annoying every time I go in there and pick it up for you.' I often use that key line: '**I know you don't realise that you're doing it**,' because in most cases other people don't realise that they're doing stuff to us that is annoying. They are doing it because to them that's their normal and not our normal.

We have to practise stopping ourselves before pointing the finger and laying blame to acknowledge that the other person probably doesn't realise they're doing something hurtful or annoying.

Watch out for those four stages that occur often in our lives. If you think of a time you experienced road rage, you most likely very quickly went through resistance, resentment, rejection and repression. Perhaps in a matter of seconds. You pushed it down in the end and continued driving …

The 4 R's can happen in a split second or you can go through them over a long period of time. But they do happen all of the time because of poor communication.

We communicate habitually, the way we have been raised and on a subconscious level that can be letting us down and making us feel frustrated in how others respond to us. Here I just want to share with you some tips on how to improve this in your relationship and parenting, from my perspective.

Let's go through the Seven Communication Secrets that we follow in our family to stay connected and not go through moments of resistance, resentment, rejection and repression.

1. *Strengths and weaknesses.* Stuart and myself have done quite a lot of personality assessments and strength assessment tests and we like to really read up on who we are as people, why we make the decisions that we make sometimes and how that works in with the whole family picture. The ones that we love are DISC and the Gallup Strengths assessment. You can look them up online and do them for yourselves and of course get your partner involved. In time of course do it on your children so that you understand who has what strengths and weaknesses in the family and why they choose to do what they choose to do at certain times.

   An example of this that really used to get us frustrated is when I would do business stuff, just like I am right now. It's 6am in LA and I'm speaking out this book. I'm doing an hour or so of business during a holiday. I enjoy that, because it gives me a sense of achievement that I've done something today towards my business and goals. It's fun for me and doesn't feel like a drag or work.

   Whereas Stuart is driven by lifestyle, which means that he generally doesn't want to touch anything while we're away and wants to be fully there, just in holiday mode, which is okay. And this used to frustrate us both, because then I would think, 'Why can't he just do an hour to make sure the business is still ticking along?' But now I'm okay with him not doing anything and he's okay with me doing a little bit of stuff, because both of us are happy in that place and we enjoy our holidays a lot more.

2. *Consistent parenting.* There isn't a good cop or bad cop in our family. There are certain rules of parenting whereby we support each other in what the kids get told, what they're allowed to do, what they're not allowed to do. Of

course resistances come up from time to time, where we might disagree in our parenting style, however, 98% of the time it is the way it is. Bedtime is bedtime. How we reprimand our children, how we educate them, what we teach them to value in life. That stays consistent and the way we look after them as well. Consistent parenting is the key, because I do see a lot of mums and dads out there who have a lot of heads butting around how to parent their children. This one is a big one to get right and agree on.

3. *Ensuring that we have our date nights and holidays.* We always book our holidays first when it comes to scheduling our year ahead and that way we have something to look forward to. We use some of the support that's around us, like my mum to schedule date nights and weekends away to go out and have some adult fun time. The kids understand that's our time and that we'll come back and hang out with them too. Having that is key and scheduling it ahead of time is important if you want it to really happen. As I always say and live by, *what gets scheduled gets done.* Even though spontaneity is a bit out the window but when you have super young children this may need to be the way it is for a little while. If you do want to stay connected and continue having a wonderful relationship, you need to make the time and schedule dates to do that.

4. *Celebrate successes.* Often people work so hard and they go through five, ten or even 20 years and when they look back they realise they haven't celebrated moments of growth and exhilaration. The entrepreneurial journey is one big roller coaster and there are moments you are going to cry, moments you are going to laugh and feel on top of the world. But the most important part is that we celebrate the successes and wins along the way and that we reward ourselves regularly. As I said before, I'm sitting here in LA writing this book and it's day one of our holiday here. We just met up with the family after an intense two-week tour around the US where I

executed all my five workshops in five cities over seven days for our Ultimate 48-Hour Author retreat that will be happening in Las Vegas at the end of a month holiday with the family. That's how we like to celebrate and reward ourselves for the successes of everything that we worked hard for over eight months to make this tour a reality. These are lifelong memories that we like to build on and look back in the future and say, 'Wow, do you remember that USA trip in 2017? And all of the things that we did and moments that we laughed.' Then discuss the funny moments and adventures we had on this trip.

5. *Be vulnerable and talk.* Everyone can put on a super strong face and especially if you're a woman reading this, one of the entrepreneurial kind, my guess is you would be a fairly strong woman. A lot of women like to think of themselves as super strong, the type who wouldn't cry and that she can handle everything that comes her way putting on the superwoman face. You can be all that, but you don't need to be that around your partner. If you're feeling sad or you're feeling down, vulnerable or scared, if you're feeling disappointed, guilty etc. – Step up and talk. Say what you're feeling. Being vulnerable will make you more connected to your partner and vice versa. Give them the space to do the same with you. Not a lot of men are willing to break down and actually say what's going on. Often at the other end of being vulnerable is the feeling of relief that you've got things out of your system and then you'll start to feel a lot better.

6. *Don't blame – Take responsibility*! Earlier I mentioned communication. I don't think that you realise that you're doing this, but this is what you're doing that is making me feel this way. Or maybe you didn't do this on purpose, but this is how this made me feel. That's often the tactic we'll take on when speaking to each other, rather than using a tone that is filled with resentment or rejection. Sometimes it's not just what words we're saying, but how we're saying it and what tone we're

using with our partners. We use the same approach when communicating with our children. I don't think you realise you're doing this, but when you do this, this is how it makes this person feel, or this is how it makes me feel. Don't blame, you're very much responsible for your communication and being understood.

7. *Watch your language!* We have been raised to communicate a certain way and often we mimic how we heard other people speak then we have subconsciously embedded certain phrases and sayings into our language. I'm going to share a few here with you to avoid. People often say, 'no problem, no drama, and no worries'. Rather than saying that, which embeds **problem, drama, worries,** what about saying, 'All **good**!', 'My **pleasure**!' I hear people say, 'I'm concerned about this, or I have concerns about this, or I'm confused'. The better thing to say here is, 'I need more **clarity** around this please'. Because the minute you use language that's more positive, your mind feels more open to receiving the answer rather than closed. Saying 'I wish', 'I hope', or 'we can't do that', or 'it's hard'. How about using things like, '**I wonder** if this is going to happen?' Or '**how** can we do that?' Or '**if** this happens'. When a lot of people say 'if this happens', very quickly after that it becomes 'then I will do that'. How about changing that to '**when** this happens?' Using **when** assumes that it is going to happen, **if** makes it uncertain. Watch your language, start to catch yourself when you say some of the un-resourceful phrases and use the opposite of what I have suggested. I have been doing that for many years now. I end up experiencing a higher quality life and results and it feels so much better to say to people the positive phrases, which makes them respond better to me.

Not all partners are made equal. Sometimes you may have a partner who's always playing the victim. If that is happening, how can you look into encouraging them to come along with you to some personal development seminars? Could you read and watch stuff together? There is a famous saying… 'Couples who grow together stay together'. And if you guys have diverging paths and you seem to be growing and he/she is not, then how can you bring them along on this journey?

I remember Stuart in the first 18 months of me starting on this journey. He wasn't as involved or hadn't learnt all the things I was learning about self-responsibility and human behaviours. We very quickly realised as we started to diverge that in order to converge we needed to start being exposed to the same information and the tips and tricks to live beyond being victims in our lives.

What about conflicting parenting styles? One parent could be a stricter person, the other more soft. That 'good cop' 'bad cop' scenario. I would encourage you if that's the case to figure out and find a happy medium. Once you discover middle ground, start setting some rules about how you will respond to certain situations so there is consistency in your approach. This way the rules guide the process, rather than your personality.

Let's link this to building your business empire:

1. Success is linked to powerful and effective communication.
2. Communication solves most problems faster than not saying anything.
3. Using empowering language will change the results you get in life.

> "Relationships fail because people take their own insecurities and try to twist them into their partner's flaws."
> Unknown

HIS ♂

How we communicate with each other has changed so quickly over the past ten years that some important skills that were the cornerstone of any relationship are vanishing and it is having disastrous effects on many entrepreneurial relationships.

The younger generations have online communications down to a tee choosing Texting, Facebook, Twitter and Snapchat to 'communicate'. What these communication platforms lack is the ability to express real feelings whether they are happiness, sadness or anger. Everything is just a hybrid of all of these emotions and I have seen many relationships mirror these.

I know that my most important relationships are with my most precious loved ones, my family. Being involved with as many things as we are, we know the importance of communicating openly, freely and honestly but we didn't always get this right, and sometimes don't to this day, but we will keep striving to each and every day.

I don't believe in perfection and although we still face our own challenges occasionally, we follow seven simple rules to keep connected and it works so I wanted to share them with you here:

1. *Understand Each Other's Strengths and Weaknesses.* Once we are clear on each other's desires and wants, assigning roles based on these is very important. In our family, Natasa is the entrepreneurial one and I am the nurturer. Is it traditional? No. Does it work? Absolutely. Until we understood this and stopped trying to change each other, things seemed forced. Now that we are both having our number one values fulfilled, mine being family and Natasa's being business, we are continuing to go from strength to strength.

2. *Take Five Minutes Every Day to Talk.* We like to call this our tea-time. Phones are out of the room and computers are off. We sit facing each other and look at each other. It would amaze you how little people look at each other when they talk these days. We talk about anything other than business. How we feel and what we would like from each other. It is a great way to connect and for men who have the biggest problem expressing their feeling, it is a perfect safe forum to do so in.

3. *Keep 'Date Night' Alive.* Life is busy hey? Finding the time to spend alone is hard but you know what, it is critical. Our schedules are crazy busy but you know what, we plan our 'date nights' at the start of the year before we plan anything else. Once it is in the diary, it happens no matter what. We get the kids a sitter, normally Natasa's mum, and we take it in turns to design the date and enjoy the time to talk and relax in each other's company.

4. *Take Regular Holidays to Re-charge and Reconnect.* At the start of the year block out time in your diary for your holidays as well. We work hard and at a very intense level. Without regular holidays we would burn out and start to feel negative. The secret here is if you don't allocate the time at the start of the year for your holidays, they simply won't happen in an entrepreneurial life. Not only does having your holidays booked give you something to look forward to, it gives you experiences that bring you closer to your spouse and the memories that will last a lifetime.

5. *Celebrate Your Successes.* Nothing brings you closer together than celebrating with your spouse. Go out to an expensive restaurant or catch a show and book a night in a hotel. Take the time to appreciate the hard work and support that you have both given each other and spend some time deciding the next goal and what the next reward will be for achieving it. We also share our successes with our children, they get a little reward for each new author that joins our program so they become involved in the celebration too.

6. *Paying it Forward With the Children.* Share you 'WHY' with your children from a young age, as they need to understand that you are part of a different world. The entrepreneurial world. The more children are spoken to, in the correct way, the better the chances they will have of being great communicators themselves. Give them choices. Keep it simple and use the classic double bind, either this or this, will improve their decision-making. Encourage your children to ask as many questions as possible and communicate openly and honesty with them.

4. *Choose a Neutral Place for any Disagreements.* There will be times when you have disagreements and when you do, it is important not to anchor these feelings in your home. If you know you need to have one of those tough conversations, take it outside or out of the house. That way, the negative feelings will not be associated with your family home. Keep these conversations flowing as even though they are tough to have, they eliminate the 'pressure build up' of emotions and the eruptions that are very common in many high-powered relationships.

The busier your lives become, the greater the need for communication and connection with each other. Make it a priority, and have that meaningful relationship that will be the envy of all of your entrepreneurial friends.

Secret Men's Only Section

This time around I want to share with you some insights into the female mind so that you can master your communication with your partner:

1. When they say, "We need to have a talk" nothing good will ever come of that. It isn't like they will then follow it up with "and I wanted to let you know that the Jet Ski you wanted can be your Christmas present." Now is the time to sit, listen and agree with everything you are being 'talked' to about.

2. When they say "I'm fine" or "there is nothing wrong" let me tell you there is and you should run for your life. Actually, don't do that, but keep the conversation going and listen for any clues as to what could be making them anxious, nervous, scared, angry etc., and let them be listened too.

3. Women can't shut off their brain like men can. We can go to our 'nothing box' and tune out to the world whereas women are constantly thinking about things and each thing they think about links to something else. So where you are watching a game of football and not thinking of anything else, they have taken that game of football that you attended last year when it was your brother's birthday to thinking why haven't you called your mum in the last month to this years unplanned Christmas lunch!

4. They talk more than us, a lot more, so understand that when they aren't talking that there is something that you have either done or not done. When this happens, suck it up and start a conversation – remember, one of the most important things for a woman is to feel that she is listened to.

5. Decide how important it is for you to win the argument. In all seriousness, what do you have to gain by pushing and pushing when most of the time, the argument isn't important at all but nasty horrible things that you might say in your emotional state could start to erode the love that was once strong.

Afterword

Thank you for spending some time with us. We trust you have picked up a few tricks that will make your business and parenting journey easier. Parenting and business have a few similarities – the beginning can be really hard but super exciting, you will have your good and bad days and both take a ton of courage to make successful. We make sacrifices in our lives for both but a testament that it doesn't have to be one or the other.

Life is never the same after you have kids or when you run a successful business. We cannot remember what life was even like as employees or people with no children. This secret club we join when we become parents and business owners is not for the faint hearted but it does build our character, patience and resilience like nothing else.

Remember the journey is the most important part, enjoy the moments: the laughs and the tears. The tears may not be enjoyable when they happen but within them lie so many lessons that you will speak of later. They are a gift as are the good times.

If you read this book it means your children are super important to you. You would never give up on your kids at the first sign of trouble and neither should you give up on your dreams and goals that your business will bring into reality.

About the Authors

Natasa started her entrepreneurial journey 7 years ago in May 2010 when Stuart made a poor decision that lost a family business overnight. With an 18-month-old son Judd, she embarked on a journey of becoming a coach. After writing her first book in 2011 her business took and reached the 6-figure mark in the following 12 months.

Stuart and Natasa had their second baby when the first book came out and juggled babies, breastfeeding and business. 2.5 years in Stuart was able to quit his day job and join the business full time. Now parents of 3 children, Judd, Mika & Xara, Natasa and Stuart run a 7-figure business from home called Ultimate 48 Hour Author.

The business has now expanded beyond Australia into the US and soon other countries around the world. Together Natasa & Stuart Denman have helped over 200 other entrepreneurs write their first books via the revolutionary Ultimate 48 Hour Author Blueprint. They live their ideal life and love raising their children together while fulfilling their purpose in life.

Natasa & Stuarts Contact Details:

Emails:
>natasa@natasadenman.com
>stuart@stuartdenman.com.au

Websites:
>www.ultimate48hourauthor.com.au
>www.natasadenman.com
>www.guiltfreeparents.com.au

IFESTYLE

FREE Ultimate Bonus

Thank you for reading our book *Guilt Free Parents*! If you loved what we shared, you might be curious what life was like before we had babies and a business. Natasa wrote her first book way before she realised that she would be a fully legit author. It was in journal form in the lead up and the first year of having her first baby Judd. It is unedited, raw and real from everything that was happening day to day and the frustrations she experienced as brand new mum.

We have it ready and available for you to download **FREE** at:

www.guiltfreeparents.com.au

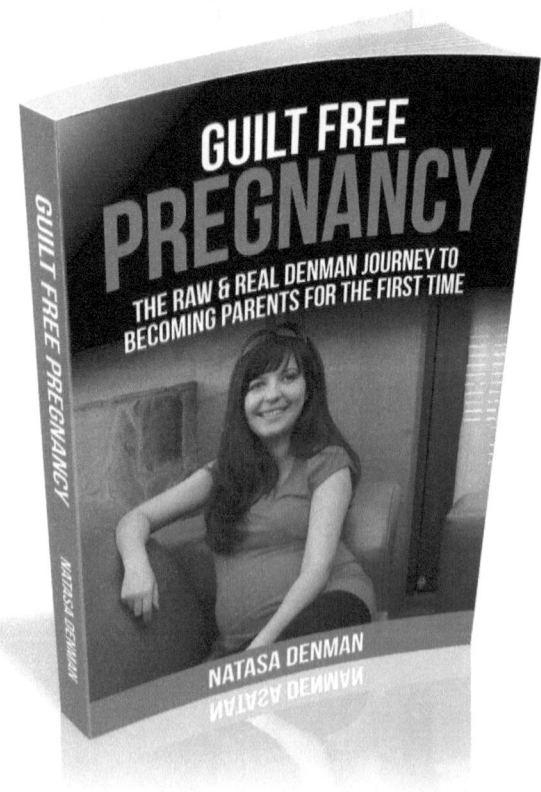

Engage Natasa to Speak at Your Next Event!

Natasa Denman is The Ultimate 48 Hour Author. A highly sought after professional speaker (CSP accredited - Certified Speaking Professional), Natasa is a 7 time published author and creator of the game changing business model, Ultimate 48 Hour Author. She has helped over 150 small business owners become first time published authors in just 3 years.

In 6 short years in business, Natasa has been nominated for The Telstra Businesswoman of the Year twice and was a finalist in AusMumpreneur of the Year in Product Innovation.

Appearing in all major media outlets across Australia Natasa is changing the way people do business in Australia and now runs a 7-figure business with her husband and 3 children traveling the country spreading her message and helping small businesses thrive.

Ultimate 48 Hour Author Blueprint for Business Success

- How to Leverage Your Business via a Book
- Lucratively Position Your Book for Success
- How to write a book in Just 48 Hours

Ultimate Brand Accelerator Formula

- How to Stand out and Thrive in Your Industry
- Hi-Touch, Hi-Tech and Hi-Fame Strategies
- The One thing that will Fast Track Your Following

1000 Days to a Million Dollar Coaching Business from Home

- How to build infrastructure for a 7 figure business
- Marketing Smarts to keep your Pipeline full
- Sales Mastery Insider Tactics

 The Sydney Morning Herald THE AGE

📞 +61 412 085 160 | ✉ natasa@natasadenman.com | 🌐 www.natasadenman.com

Ultimate 48 Hour Author

The journey to our business success began with the writing of Natasa's first book – The 7 Ultimate Secrets to Weight Loss. This was the turning point and has continued to be the backbone to our business – authoring books ourselves and helping hundreds so far do it for themselves.

Attendance at an Ultimate 48 Hour Author Retreat is only permitted upon successful qualification. Not everyone that wants to write a book is a good match for our program. We do not work with fiction or children's books.

Ideally first you should attend one of our signature workshops called: Ultimate 48 Hour Author Blueprint for Business Success.

We run these in all major cities around Australia a couple of times per year and almost monthly in Melbourne – our home city. We have now started taking these in the US and other countries. The retreats are based in Melbourne for Australia and start at 2pm on a Friday and end 2pm on the Sunday.

To find out when our next Ultimate 48 Hour Author Blueprint for Business Success is running near you – go to the Events Tab on **www.ultimate48hourauthor.com.au/events**.

Mention you saw this in the Guilt Free Parents books and we will grant you a discounted ticket of $30 instead of $49. Just email us for a discounted link. You will also receive a paperback copy of the *Ultimate 48 Hour Author* book on arrival at the workshop.

If you cannot make it to one of our Live events here is a link to a **FREE Training: www.ultimate48hourauthor.com.au/webinar**.

To check out how everything unfolds at the Ultimate 48 Hour Author Retreat watch our awesome Experience video here: **http://bit.ly/Ultimate48HourAuthor**.

Ultimate 48 Hour Author Packages

	Silver	Gold	Remote
Mentoring & Accountability			
2 Hour Pre Weekend Prep Session One on One	✓	✓	✓
Unlimited Email Support	✓	✓	✓
Laser Mentoring until Book Release	✓	✓	✓
Ultimate 48 Hour Author Weekend Training & Support:	✓	✓	Recording
1. Speaking Success System	✓	✓	
2. The Power of Social Media	✓	✓	
3. Connecting Through Video	✓	✓	
4. Free Publicity Generation	✓	✓	
5. Successful Publicity Follow Up System	✓	✓	
6. Pre-Launch Campaign	✓	✓	
7. Your Mindset Success	✓	✓	
Essentials for Success	✓	✓	
Luxury Accommodation - 2 Nights Check out 10am Sunday	✓	✓	
Restaurant Style Meals	✓	✓	
Transcription of Your Book - 5 Hours Max		✓	✓
Webinar Set Up and Promotion to Explode Your Book Sales		✓	✓
Checklists, Templates & Guides for Your Success		✓	✓
Publishing Package		✓	✓
ISBN/Barcode for both Book and E-book		✓	✓
Copyediting (40 000 words max)		✓	✓
Internal Layout & Design		✓	✓
Cover Creation (Including 3D Version)		✓	✓
500 Books (Black and White internal printing)		✓	✓
Professional Author Photoshoot		✓	✓
E-book Version of the Book		✓	✓
Library Deposit of Your Book		✓	✓
Amazon Upload of Your Book		✓	✓
Graphic Design Jump Start Package		✓	✓
Mock 3D Image of the book - Created before weekend		✓	✓
Logo Design (Business or Personal Brand)		✓	✓
Facebook Cover Photo		✓	✓
Pull Up Banner Design		✓	✓
Business Cards Design (Front and Back)		✓	✓
Live Training Support		✓	✓
Ultimate Social Media Masterclass 2 Days 9-5	✓	✓	Recording
Ultimate Sales Mastery Masterclass 2 days 9-5	✓	✓	Recording
Ultimate Bums on Seats Masterclass 2 Days 9-5	✓	✓	Recording
Online Support			
Ultimate Business Support Inner Circle Membership (12 months)	✓	✓	✓
Bums on Seats Online Course with Francesca Moi	✓	✓	✓
Library of over 100 Hours of Filmed Footage on Marketing & Sales	✓	✓	✓

Natasa Denman's Other Books ...

Available to purchase on
www.natasadenman.com

Check out some of our Ultimate 48 Hour Authors ...

Check out some of our Ultimate 48 Hour Authors ...

Check out some of our Ultimate 48 Hour Authors ...

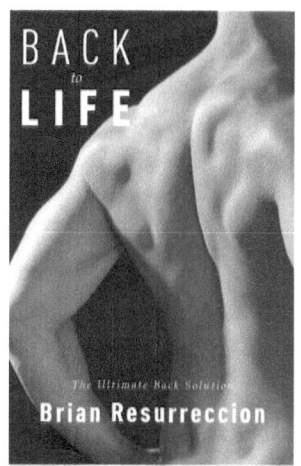

Check out some of our Ultimate 48 Hour Authors ...

www.ingramcontent.com/pod-product-compliance
Lightning Source LLC
Chambersburg PA
CBHW021107080526
44587CB00010B/418